Behind the Family Mask:

Therapeutic Change in Rigid Family Systems

by

Maurizio Andolfi,
Claudio Angelo, Paolo Menghi,
and Anna Maria Nicolò-Corigliano
Family Therapy Institute of Rome

Translated by Claire L. Chodorkoff

BRUNNER/MAZEL, *Publishers* • New York

THIRD PRINTING

Library of Congress Cataloging in Publication Data
Main entry under title:

Behind the family mask.

Bibliography: p.
Includes index.
1. Family psychotherapy.   2. Rigidity (Psychology)
I. Andolfi, Maurizio.
RC488.5.B4   1983   616.89'156   82-22817
ISBN 0-87630-330-0

Copyright © 1983 by Maurizio Andolfi

Published by
BRUNNER/MAZEL
19 Union Square West
New York, New York 10003

MANUFACTURED IN THE UNITED STATES OF AMERICA

Foreword

The initiation of change within families must be an interactive phenomenon. Andolfi and his colleagues of the Rome Family Institute
have developed a unique pragmatic and esthetic system — professionally personal and personally professional invasive warfare with the family system. They aim to force flexibility so the inspissated self-rescue efforts of the family may be altered. They actually teach the family creativity by being themselves creative.

The authors have also expanded the family metaphor by themselves
being a metaphor for a self-actualizing (normal) family. In dramatic
contrast with the usual effort to acculturate the family, they oppose
each rigid family's delusional metaphor or fragment thereof with an interactive nonrational metaphor. They actually create a live metaphor
out of each time/space and person/setting.

The authors do not assume pathology is the essential problem. They assume the original pathology has been massively complicated by the inevitable family struggle for recovery; the therapist's problem is like that of the surgeon after an attack of peritonitis—he must first cut away the scar tissue which strangulates the intestine before he can cut out the 12 inches of cancerous tissue. The therapist may displace the scapegoat, reduce father's isolation, or metaphorically pathologize a phobic mother. He may even use himself as a provocative instrument to destabilize the family system with tenderness. This unique new crisis thereby empowers the next larger system, which includes the therapeutic team.

This group may have also put a finger on the one way to become an experienced professional without the usual devastating "burn-out" that follows when the poor therapist ends up being the Jonah to one "whale" of a family after another. Even if the "whale" vomits you out again the stress leaves one exhausted and phobic about whaling expeditions. The compulsive therapist will object to the freedom necessitated by this method but a compulsive therapist shouldn't go near families—they will drive him crazy.

In essence these authors have planted a creative seed that may start a revolution. Our previous United Nations "talking" game is mostly impotent. The Rome group has learned to use creativity to empower the family. If successful, there emerges an intrafamilial peace treaty that could include an endless series of new metaphors. Such a family could be truly self-actualizing. Imagine a normal family loose in our world!

Carl A. Whitaker, M.D.

Contents

Preface

This volume represents the evolution of the work of the Institute of Family Therapy of Rome over a span of eight years.

In our earliest phase, which coincided with our personal search for shared ideas and objectives, we found it useful to adopt a "structural" theoretical model. This gave us a framework allowing for the refinement and simplification of reality, separating the family unit into its significant subsystems. Our model of therapy was founded on the teachings of Salvador Minuchin, who stresses the importance of observing the actions as they unfold as part of the therapeutic scenario. We believed, with him, that diagnosis and intervention were not separate operations, but, in fact, essential ingredients of the therapeutic process.

After this initial period, our attention moved beyond the treatment of mild and moderate disturbances in children and adolescents to more serious and chronic pathologies. In this volume these will be referred to as "rigid family systems." In this second phase we came to realize that the significance or function of the disturbed behavior was often deeply hidden. This gave us the impetus to move toward a much more complex sphere of research.

We passed from listening to the language of mildly disturbed children to hearing the language of the psychotic. While certain similarities between the two were evident, the language of the psychotic seemed to us to be richer with metaphoric implications, more difficult to interpret, and, above all, incompatible with our wish to assimilate it into our logic. Our continuous and repeated failure in attempting to achieve "change at any cost" opened the way to new considerations. We began to ask ourselves how useful it really was to think of irrationality, contradiction, violence, and exclusion as defects which must be corrected. We further asked whether these qualities might not be interpreted, rather, as elements designed to set up a relationship which, however incongruous and dysfunctional at one level, might be seen as congruous and functional at another level.

Peering behind the family façade, we came to understand that menacing and openly attacking the systemic equilibrium consolidated by the family over time could only result in reinforcing the stability of the family fortress. If, in the newly formed therapeutic system, we ourselves would assume the responsibility for being the guardians of the family's homeostasis, we might be able to free the family from the responsibility of fighting off our attempts to change. In other words, if we became more rigid, it might permit the family to become more flexible.

This idea derived from a line of paradoxical thinking which started with Watzlawick, developed with Haley, and found, with Selvini-Palazzoli and her colleagues, an even more sophisticated clinical application with families involved in schizophrenic transactions.

In a third phase the attempt to understand and utilize the complexity of the family's world in a therapeutic sense stimulated us to search more deeply into each component of the therapeutic system. Considering each member's *function* as the special point where the individual and the system connect, we began to pay greater attention to the intricate interaction between the tasks and the roles which the family system assigns to its members.

More recently, the teachings of Carl Whitaker have been particularly illuminating for us. He has affirmed our efforts at searching for a therapeutic metareality in which the individual potential of each participant might be rediscovered.

This book is the result of the developmental evolution described above. It is also the point of departure for new research on the individual observed in his personal process of development within the family.

The clinical material in the book was furnished primarily by Maurizio Andolfi. Theoretical elaborations and the overall organization resulted from the challenges and dynamic exchanges among the four authors. Their intention was to present a body of ideas structured as an organic whole.

The principal points of a coherent therapeutic process demonstrating our conceptual presuppositions are expressed in Chapter 7. Katia Giacometti, who was an integral part of our exchange, was responsible for shaping this chapter.

We are especially grateful to our students in training at the Institute of Family Therapy of Rome. They sustained us and encouraged our efforts at developing the ideas expressed in this book. We also thank our many colleagues on the staff who, even beyond giving us advice and counsel, had to bear with the manifestations of our creative anxiety.

A special acknowledgment must go to Carmine Saccu who, though not an actual participant in the writing of this book, was beside us through all the pangs of our development, stimulating and enriching our ideas with his own clinical experience.

Final thanks go to Marcella de Nichilo, who, with her competent, critical mind, edited and revised the original manuscript, and to Claire L. Chodorkoff, who translated the manuscript into English.

Behind the Family Mask:

Therapeutic Change in
Rigid Family Systems

CHAPTER 1

The Individual and the Family: Two Systems in Evolution

Although the family is the unit of observation on which we base our research,* we are primarily interested in individual human beings and the complexity of their behavior, as seen through an understanding of their development in the family. The essential link between *individual needs* and *social demands* has compelled us to integrate diverse interpretative modalities of human behavior.

Consequently, on one hand, we have been driven to observe the family as a *relational system* that goes beyond the individual and that articulates among its members various individual components, applying

---

*The term *research* in this context implies more of a theoretical search than an empirical investigation. (Translator's note)

to the family those principles that are generally used for open systems (Andolfi, 1979). On the other hand, we have put at the center of the study of the family *the individual and his/her process of differentiation,* as postulated by Bowen (1978) and Whitaker and Malone (1981). Rather than emphasizing the differences between the individual and relational approaches, differences that have been overemphasized by most family therapy theorists, we have used the relational method for a better understanding of human behavior and its evolutionary cycle.

It is probable that, in the attempt to integrate different vocabularies and methods, instead of simplifying things, we may have complicated them unduly. However, it seems to us that it is worth running this risk in order to reach our fundamental objective, i.e., to furnish a dynamic vision of the individual in the family context.

PROCESS OF DIFFERENTIATION WITHIN THE FAMILY SYSTEM

We start with the assumption that the family is *an active system in constant transformation,* that is, a complex organism that changes over time to ensure continuity and psychosocial growth in its component members. This dual process of continuity and growth allows the development of the family as a unit and at the same time assures the differentiation of its members.

The *need for differentiation,* understood as the necessity of self-expression for each individual, is meshed with the *need for cohesiveness* and maintenance of unity in the group over time. Ideally, the individual is guaranteed membership in a family group which is sufficiently cohesive and from which he/she can differentiate progressively and individually, becoming less and less dependent in his/her functioning on the original family system, until he/she can separate and institute, on his/her own, with different functions, a new system.

Various authors have described a gradual progression in the psychological development of the individual from a state of fusion/undifferentiation to a state of ever greater separation and individuation. This route is determined not only by biological stimuli and the interaction of the psychological mother and child (Mahler, 1952), but also by the interactive processes inside the system, particularly the family system.

Some theorists, such as Bowen (1978), consider the family imprint so determining that the level of individual autonomy can be predicted very early on, even in infancy. Also, the course of future individual history can be predicted on the basis of the level of differentiation of the parents and the emotional climate prevailing in the family of origin.

The structural connectedness that helps determine individual autonomy in each family member is made up of the triangular relationship between parents and child, in which one component, represented in turn by each of the three parties, constitutes the external reference point, the bottom-line confrontation for whatever transaction may transpire between the other two parties. Indeed, in a dyadic, exclusive relationship it is not possible for differentiation to take place if neither of the two parties involved is able to establish a relationship with a third party. It would be as if a navigator attempted to find his position by using only one point of reference. Even in relationships which may be apparently dyadic—as, for example, in couples or in families in which only one parent is present—one must realize that each is part of a network of relationships which involve respective families of origin. From these, innumerable triangles are formed, which are reflected in intimate relationships. The vicissitudes which every family experiences in the making and the unmaking of its relational triangles influence the evolution of its structure. Through interactions which allow each one to experiment with what is and is not permissible in the relationship, the basis of a systemic unity is created. Structure is shaped by the relationships within this unique system and open to new formulations and adaptations, responding to the changing needs of each member of the system, as well as to the group as a whole. The possibility of varying the relational modality allows each one the opportunity to test new parts of himself, reflecting the degree of differentiation acquired.

We may assume that, to achieve differentiation—to find *personal space,* one's own identity—each person will expand and delimit through exchanges with others. This identity may be enriched to the degree that the individual tries and learns new relational modes which allow him to vary the functions he serves within the subsystems without losing his own continuity even in moments of evolution with different protagonists (Menghi, 1977).

The capacities to change, to move from one place to another, to participate, to separate, to belong to diverse subsystems all permit the possibility of serving unique functions, of exchanging and acquiring new ones, and of thereby expressing other, more differentiated aspects of oneself. This process of separation-individuation requires the family to pass through phases of disorganization, as the equilibrium of one stage is disrupted in preparation for moving to a more suitable one. During periods of instability, the balance of family cohesion and differentiation among individual family members is challenged anew. These phases of instability, characterized by confusion and uncertainty, mark the passage toward new functional equilibrium. This can happen only *if the family is able to bear the increase in diversity among its members.*

An analogy with biological phenomena may seem surprising, but, in fact, the components of a system behave like the cells of an organism in the course of embryonic evolution. From an undifferentiated and confused whole, based on information coming from the nucleus and surrounding tissues, the cell develops progressively into a specific organ composed of cells with differing characteristics and functions. The function thus comes to have a dual nature: It is a characteristic of that cell but it is also the product of interactions with other cells and with its genetic endowment. Similarly, in the evolution of a person through an ongoing exchange of behavior and information, each individual, differentiating himself or herself, acquires a specific identity and unique functions which evolve over time. These functions, which members of a system have tacitly negotiated, allow the system to adapt to changes and to let relationships unfold. The change in functions of one member of the system brings simultaneous change in the complementary functions of the others and characterizes both the growth process of the individual and the continual reorganization of the family system through its life-cycle.

This evolution, however, may not occur. It may happen that the rules of association and communication which govern the family system prevent individuation and the autonomy of single members. This lack of autonomy, seen in the inability to alter functions over a period of time, results in persons who coexist only at the level of functions, i.e., each one is forced to live only as a function of the others. In this situation each one faces the difficulty of affirming and recognizing his own identity, along with that of the others. No one can ever freely choose to elaborate certain functions or to break away. Each finds himself/herself forced to be always that which the system imposes.

In a system in which specific expectations about each one's role or function preexist, the individuation of each member will encounter strong obstacles. If, for example, parents force a child to constantly behave like a mature person, demanding adult-like performances, the child must make the effort to meet their demand. His attempt is the price to pay for maintaining a relationship very dear to him. The final result, however, is a progressive *alienation in his assigned function*. In fact, the imbalance between the performance requested and the child's emotional immaturity makes his behavior an empty recitation. The situation ultimately is exacerbated when he is presented with requests contradictory to behaving like an adult, for example, to remain a child and not reach sexual maturity. Inevitably, differentiation is more difficult in those areas where there is a conflict in demands or where demands are highly inappropriate to the individual's level of maturity.

If the *function* represents the spectrum of behaviors which meet reciprocal needs within a relationship, it is evident how it may assume a *positive* or *negative* connotation, depending on the types of families being considered. In families which foster both family cohesion and individuation of family members, each person develops a stable, differentiated image of himself, of other family members, and of himself in respect to the others. Each one knows that he can share his personal space with the others without feeling forced to exist only as a function of them. As long as family encounters result in mutual enrichment, they are not perceived and experienced as intrusions but rather as real interchanges in which each one gives and receives at the same time.

On the other hand, the function assumes a negative connotation if it is assigned rigidly and irreversibly and when it contradicts biological function, as, for example, in a case where the paternal function is assigned to a son rather than to the father. This causes the progressive alienation of the individual most involved, with concomitant damage to his *self* and to his personal space. When this process tends to become irreversible, rigid, and undifferentiated, a pathological situation results. If the son assumes the function of the father not in a moment of particular need, but consistently, that function will become a cage for him as well as for other family members. In these cases each one becomes a creator and a victim of the same "functional trap." The absence of clear interpersonal boundaries which results from this type of relationship is translated into the impossibility of either freely entering an intimate relationship or breaking away.

Constantly maintaining a safe distance and, contrariwise, entering into a fused relationship are the behaviors most common to these systems, where personal space is confounded with interactive space, the individual with the function he serves, *being for one self* with *being as a function of the other.* The only possibility for coexistence may then become the intrusion into the personal space of others, accompanied by the loss of one's own personal space. At first protectiveness, indifference, refusal, victimization, even madness become individual attributes, which grow into stereotypical roles in an unalterable script. The more this relational mode becomes the *principal or only mode possible, the more rigid the system becomes.* The vital need to live in terms of reciprocal function makes for increasingly sterile exchanges and for ever more indefinite boundaries with personal space constantly reduced until it becomes confused with interactive space.

The members of these families may be compared to a series of boxes. Immersed in a liquid, they remain afloat only if they are soldered together with their surface presenting a continuity (see Figure 1). If, one box manages to break loose with its boundaries free, the others may risk sinking (see Figure 2).

In these situations the primary concern of the individual is not so much how to bring about self-differentiation (this is much too ambitious an idea) as it is the fear that someone else will delineate his own "autonomy before I am able to build mine." It is clear that the fundamental guiding rule in a system where these mechanisms apply is the impossibility of "leaving the field." The necessity of continuously checking that no one succeeds in clearly defining himself or herself arises because this would be perceived as an act of independence translated as betrayal. Once the rules of the game are learned, along with the clear notion that they are immutable, it becomes quite possible to substitute players. Even when new components of the system are selected, for example, a mate or new friends, they are only those who guarantee that they will not disturb or interfere with the previously learned rules; those who do not offer this security are excluded (Piperno, 1979).

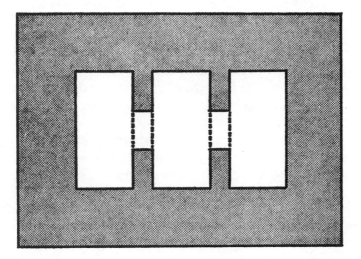

Figure 1

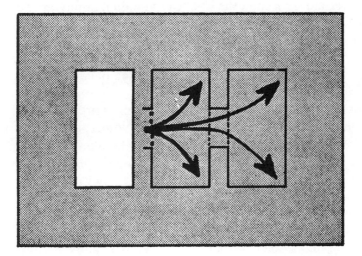

Figure 2

A HYPOTHESIS FOR CHANGE:
FLEXIBILITY AND RIGIDITY IN A SYSTEM

In healthy families individual differentiation and group cohesion are guaranteed by the dynamic equilibrium established between the mechanisms of diversification and those of stabilization. The former are directed toward increasing the variability of interaction, while the latter are directed toward consolidating and affirming known solutions. One may posit, therefore, that the process of change and the evolutionary passage from one stage to another are promoted by variations in the relationship between the forces moving toward change and those maintaining homeostasis, with greater energy favoring change. Every change and consequent resettling will, therefore, be preceded by a temporary imbalance within the relationship. This imbalance will be in direct proportion to the significance and scope of the change and consequent restabilization (Andolfi et al., 1980).

The family may be seen as a *system in constant transformation,* evolving by virtue of its capacity to weaken its own stability and then retrieve it through a reorganization of its structure with new bases. The family as an open system experiences pressures toward change both internally, through the roles of individual family members meeting the exigencies of their life-cycle, and externally, through societal demands (Andolfi, 1979). The internal and external pulls and the consequent need for change require that the family members continually assess their relationships and reevaluate the balance between family unity and individual growth.

This process is influenced by past as well as present experiences of the family unit and each of its members. Numerous levels of interaction are simultaneously present within the family. These may be seen as that of the couple, that of the nuclear family, that of the extended family, and that of the individual members as they experience the larger world around them. If we accept this premise, it is not possible to analyze the disengagement of an adolescent without considering that when he finds new external functions, inevitably, changes in his personal space induce changes in the personal space and emotional interaction of his parents, as well as between each parent and his or her respective parents. In fact, a family system is not a simple two-dimensional reality; rather, it is a tri-dimensional one in which past family relationships become manifest in the present in order to develop in the future (Bowen, 1978).

In families where any change in the relationships is perceived as threatening, a progressive rigidifying of the present interactional scheme and of each member's function is seen. Roles become crystallized in stereotypical interrelationships, with the concomitant avoidance of new and differentiated experiences and information.

The flexibility and/or rigidity of a system are not characteristics intrinsic to its structure; rather, they seem linked to the dynamism and variability possible within a defined time and space. They can be seen as a function of the capacity to tolerate a temporary disorganization with a view toward a new stability. For example, a system which is flexible at stage A might become rigid at stage B or stage C. (Andolfi et al., 1980).

In this sense one may theorize that individual pathology may develop in relation to intersystemic or intrasystemic pressure upon a particular entity, corresponding to the evolutionary phase of the family. This pathology serves to maintain the equilibrium and functioning that the system has achieved. Through this device, the system may change in order not to change at all (Ashby, 1956); that is, it may use the new input to adopt surface changes which neither modify nor question its functioning.

We have already stated that every change, whether intrasystemic (the birth of a child, children leaving home, menopause, death of a family member, divorce, etc.) or intersystemic (job transfer, family move, change in working conditions, deep crisis of values, etc.), seriously impinges upon the functioning of the family. Change requires a process of adaptation which may be seen as a modification in the rules of association in order to insure family cohesion while allowing space for the psychological growth of the individual family members (Andolfi, 1979).

One reaction to the specter of change, which is perceived as traumatic to the entire system, is to select a family member to carry the stress and tension of this perception through the expression of a symptomatology. Among the families who select this route, two types may be clearly distinguished: 1) families at risk, and 2) rigid families.

Families at Risk

In these families, identification of a "patient" represents a temporary response to a new event, a tentative, undefined solution. The symptomatic behavior of the selected, identified family member serves to focus all the tension upon him or her at a time when the stability of the entire group appears in danger. In assigning to the identified patient the temporary function of keeping the system stable and cohesive, the others may then shape and integrate their functions in relation to him. Let us clarify this with an example.

The death of the maternal grandfather, with a consequent move of the grandmother into the daughter's nuclear family household, may produce tensions which affect three generations at diverse levels. A difficult period of adaptation is required. If the imbalance caused by the new family member is seen as a threat to the stability of the system, it is possible that a child—perhaps a child with some organic disturbance, ideally suited to regenerate protective patterns—will manifest regression, refusing to go to school and demonstrating infantile and tyrannical behavior at home. The subsequent tension may then be conveniently focused upon the symptomatic behavior of the child and grandmother may finally find her space in the system "for the good of the grandchild." For example, the child might move into grandmother's room, leaving that of an older brother, so that she can keep an eye on him and see that he sleeps well. The parents, worrying about the behavior of their child, are not forced to choose between two loyalties: that between the spouses which excludes the grandmother and that between mother and daughter which excludes daughter's husband. The behavior of the child acts as a safety valve for the couple, who can then protect their marital harmony. The older brother, meanwhile, can feel more autonomous out of the house while still serving his limited function within the children's subsystem. If the distance between his grown-up behavior and the infantile behavior of his younger brother is widened by the needs of the parents, he will not be able to meet his personal needs of adolescence. The identified patient, for his part, is ready to sacrifice part of his autonomy to fill the selected function of focusing upon himself all the interactional difficulties of the family.

The designation of "patient" may fluctuate from one person to another within the family, or the symptomatology may have varied expressions. A certain amount of flexibility permits the family to experiment with alternative functions through the reversibility of their normal-pathological relationships. But if this reversible and temporary mechanism of identification does not, in fact, result in assuring the family satisfying structural order, the risk is that it may become a rigid mechanism wherein the identity of the identified patient, as well as of the other family members, is progressively replaced by highly predictable, repetitive functions. In this transformation from a fluctuating to a fixed designation, external influences weigh heavily. These may act as reinforcement for the family in the inevitability of its solutions.

Therapy is often requested in this phase of transition—i.e., when the risk seems to be evolving into undeniable certitude. At this moment therapeutic intervention may favor a rediscovery of the vital potential within a rigidified family group. However, therapy, like any external input, may reinforce the stasis of the family, becoming in part responsible for the family's further deterioration.

Rigid Families

In rigid families the passage from one evolutionary stage to the next may be perceived as catastrophic. The necessity for change becomes transmuted into the adopting of a known solution, applied in the present and "programmed" for the future. The family is closed to any experimentation and new learning (Watzlawick et al., 1974). A solution which had served in one phase is rigidly applied in others. There is a twofold result when predictable, unchanging solutions are applied. On one hand, the relationship between personal and interactive space is locked in, making identity and function coincide; on the other hand, individual and family life-cycle is arrested in a phase which corresponds to the overlearned solution.

In these families the designation of "patient" becomes irreversible and indispensable, not only for avoiding the risk of instability at that specific stage but also for avoiding successive evolution of the family. The identified family member who must function as the homeostatic regulator finds himself no longer adequate to the exigencies of the moment.

Thus, a dissociative symptom, anorexia, or depressive behavior may be programmed to face the threat of momentary instability, such as the emancipation of a child, as well as in preparation for the distancing of other children, or the death of a parent with the consequent functional void produced by such an event. In this case the designation changes from fluctuating to fixed, producing a progressive crystallization of the symptomalogical function of the identified patient and of the interrelational functioning of the other family members.

This process of stabilization uses systemic energy for maintaining rigid functions which limit exchanges to redundant interactional schemes. In this way a "pathology-function," always increasingly irreversible in one family member, finds its counterpart, "health-function," comparably irreversible in the others. This stasis permeates the relationship between the system and the external world, whose influence will be filtered and used to maintain the accustomed equilibrium.

In exploring the double significance of the symptomatic behavior, we see that on one side it represents a transformation in the functioning of cohesion and on the other it is a sign of the pain and suffering resulting from the restrictions imposed on every member of the system. There is an attempt to blend the contradictory aspects of family reality, to "freeze" the conflict between the tendencies directed toward maintenance and those directed toward rupturing the acquired equilibrium. In this attempt, the symptom may be interpreted as a "metaphor" of instability and as an indicative sign of the fragility of the system. For this reason the utilization of the symptoms must become one of the priorities of intervention early on in therapy (Andolfi & Angelo, 1981).

CHAPTER 2

The Diagnosis: Hypotheses to Be Tested in the Intervention

FAMILY SYSTEM AND THERAPEUTIC SYSTEM

If we evaluate the rigidity or flexibility of a family system, viewing the therapist as an "external," neutral observer of objective phenomena, the family's repetitive and stereotypical patterns of interaction will appear to be the material on which to base intervention.

However, a totally different perspective may emerge if we observe the *suprasystem family-therapists,* which results from the interaction between the two respective subsystems in the context of the intervention (Selvini-Palazzoli, 1980). A point of view which includes the entire therapeutic system forces us to reformulate the concept of diagnosis and change. In this view observation is focused both on the functional intertwining of the family and on the role assigned by them to the therapist, who inevitably becomes an equal, active element in a system which includes them all. Part of the diagnostic process, therefore, must be directed to evaluating where and how to focus the therapeutic intervention and how it will be utilized by the family (Haley, 1976). Family members may adopt it to reinforce, once again, their own structure, forming a familiarly rigid therapeutic system; or the intervention of the therapist may act as a *destabilizing input,* disturbing their rigidity, causing a redistribution of the functions and capacities of each individual. The diagnosis depends on the ability of the therapist to assess the interaction, which co-involves him, as an outside observer might. He must be a musician who plays in the orchestra but also conducts it. To achieve a successful performance it is essential that the orchestra follow him, but he must not be so tied to that function that he cannot use his instrument to the optimum in the development of the musical theme.

The therapist encounters three problems: The first involves the necessity of *isolating the function that the family wishes to impose upon him.* As many parents-to-be anticipate the task and function of their unborn child, so the family imagines what the task and function of the therapist should be even before treatment begins. If the therapist wishes to be free of meeting this expectation, he must be able to clearly delimit his boundaries in respect to those of the family by immediately facing this in defining the therapeutic situation (Whitaker, 1975).

The second difficulty lies in searching out the definitions and images related to the functions of each family member. As a detective, he uncovers the role of each character in a plot which he must further. This serves to help him enter into the dilemmas in the life-style of the family. He is not yet ready to delineate the ties, the rules, or the "true" functions assigned, but he is in the process of constructing "his own truth" in the therapeutic context, which will shake that "truth" already programmed by the family. Through his perception of the family-therapist interaction, he *creates a new reality* together with the family.

The third difficulty is related to the necessity of evaluating the intensity, i.e., *the degree of force invested in his destabilizing input* which will break up the rigid patterns and still be acceptable to the family. Much depends on the family's response to the image which the therapist suggests after having explored certain contextual elements as they have emerged during their interaction. From the mass of verbal and nonverbal information gathered, the therapist selects those elements which hold most significance. These are elements which refer to the observed interactions, attitudes, or behaviors which were ambiguous and contradictory in nature. The therapist can quite simply select an image of the family which differs from the habitual one. Both verbal and nonverbal contextual information can be highly significant because of the differing perceptions among family members. It is precisely through countering the image furnished by the family with an alternative that the therapist is able to release the tension which sustains the therapeutic process.

With this perspective, even the gathering of information for diagnostic purposes takes on a new structure. Questions which give a confused mass of relevant and irrelevant information are replaced with those directed toward information which reveals the tendency for cohesion and for differentiation in the system. The new reality which is created becomes the frame of reference for the definition of the relationships within the therapeutic system. If the family continues to raise problems tied to its usual, habitual image, the therapist must create an alternative image which can break the circuit of redundancy in which the family system flounders.

The therapist must use this new image, then, as a destabilizing input in order to see how the system reacts. The family's responses to this therapeutic intervention, together with the therapist's ability to initiate change, give strong clues about the degree of rigidity. The danger that the family may reabsorb the intervention forces us to refine our diagnostic hypothesis continually rather than stay with one definition. At each point, we must be able to support our hypothesis, at least partially (Selvini-Palazzoli, 1980). We need not take it as a truth, but we must use it to draw out possibilities and alternatives already present in the system which can lead to new understanding. The therapist introduces alternatives and the element of surprise, but it is the family which will "justify" the diagnostic hypothesis through an internal reorganization, using abilities and values already present in its existential endowment.

Let us clarify this concept by describing factors we assume lead a family into therapy and then giving a range of possible therapeutic responses to the expectations of the family system.

In families where developmental processes are experienced as threatening, interactional patterns and individual functions become progressively rigidified until, ultimately, individual pathology is expressed. The greater the system's need for stability, the greater the severity and irreversibility of the resulting pathology. In other words, the system reorganizes itself so that it will not have to change. Roles, functions, relations, and interactive space become more rigid. To counteract the stress inherent in developmental change, the system substitutes the stress evoked by the symptomatic behavior of one family member, the identified patient, around which the anxieties of all family members revolve (Nicolò & Saccu, 1979). The identified patient thus represents both the impossibility of change and the only possibility of change. His behavior, with its contradictory aspects, has the effect of congealing processes which are moving in opposite directions while providing the possibility for new input, i.e., the therapeutic intervention. Simultaneously serving as both guardian of the system's stability and agent of systemic disruption, the identified patient's behavior represents a metaphor for the dilemma of a family that would like to move while standing still.

In the light of this premise, we can more easily understand the contradictions that the family brings to therapy, since the request for therapy is motivated by this same dilemma. Consequently, when a new element, the therapist, is introduced, he is expected to accept the family's paradoxical request by helping them to move while standing still (Angelo, 1981).

To grasp the complexity of the therapeutic situation, it is important to recognize that in rigid family systems the members become increasingly incapable of owning their own conflicts and contradictions (for example, concerning change and immobility, dependence and separation). These conflicts appear so threatening that they have to be neutralized by skillfully distributing their constituent parts within the family. Accordingly, each member adopts a vision of reality complementary to that of another; there is the sick member and the healthy one, the aggressor and the victim, the wise one and the incompetent one, with increasingly rigid rules determining when and where the respective functions are fulfilled.

Within the family some member represents the tendency toward movement while another personifies the tendency to stand still; in a similar way the family predetermines the parts to be assigned to the therapist in the new therapeutic structure. The therapist, too, has to play a part in the family script, not as a whole person, but as another actor on whom some of the functions originally "impersonated" by someone in the family are projected (Andolfi & Angelo, 1981). In the therapeutic interaction the family's objective remains the same: *to separate into constituent parts those contradictions which each member is afraid to experience at a personal level.*

Telephone contacts by a family member, letters of presentation, the direct or indirect mediation of other professionals, institutions, or friends of the family represent some of the apparently neutral means the family uses to program in advance the rules of the therapeutic relationship and the parts that each person will play. The more rigid the relational script of the family, the more assiduous it will be in this effort. The family will try to pigeonhole the therapist, fitting him into its own framework of rules and functions even before meeting him.

If what the family really fears is change, and not the contrary, then the identified patient and his or her family members will present a united front in proposing a program for therapy that will not disturb the equilibrium they have acquired. If the therapist accepts their program, or gets drawn into it, he will inevitably reinforce the family's static-pathological tendencies. We are convinced that many therapists fall into playing the part the family "assigns" to them, not only because of inexperience but also to satisfy needs similar to those of the family — that is, the therapist's need to program highly stable relationships that will not threaten *his own security* (Andolfi, 1979).

When this occurs, the family does not learn anything substantially new. It merely utilizes its own dysfunctional patterns in a more refined way, maintaining intact the roles assigned to each member. The result is a progressive impoverishment of personal "identity," which is gradually replaced by repetitive and highly predictable functions (Piperno, 1979). In a context of this type, the function of the therapist is equally repetitive and predictable, for he, too, is afraid to change and to discover new parts of himself to utilize in his relations with others.

In other cases, it is the setting of the therapeutic encounter that rigidly defines the rules of the context and the parts to be played, preventing both family and therapist from uncovering important parts of their own selves to invest in the therapeutic relationship. This is commonly the case in institutions where interventions are based on premises of "welfare," that is, where therapy is defined as doing something for or in place of someone else (whether an individual or a group) who presents himself or is described as helpless (Barrows, 1981).

It is clear, then, that we can evaluate a therapeutic situation using the same criteria of flexibility that we apply to a family system. We consider a therapeutic system flexible if it can alter its own systemic equilibrium so that the relation between functions (of therapist and family) and individuation can be modified in the process of therapy. Contrarily, a therapeutic system becomes rigid (this can occur during any phase of treatment) if it fails to offer its members the possibility of freeing themselves from static expectations and functions and of moving toward more integrated levels of functioning and greater differentiation (Andolfi et al., 1980).

The Utilization of Familial Defenses

An initial goal of intervention is to make the family's problem become the problem of the therapeutic system, and consequently to have the therapist share in the difficulties that previously belonged exclusively to the family. We will now describe specifically how this occurs and why *this redefinition of the therapeutic relationship represents an initial "therapeutic" response to the contradictory expectations of rigid families.*

The therapist's first problem is how to engage a family that simultaneously presents contradictory requests, without getting enmeshed in the family's paradoxical mechanisms. In fact, the family is prepared either to sabotage his efforts if he takes the initiative or to force him to attempt the impossible if he declares that the situation is hopeless.

Experience has taught us that the first step is not learning how to defend oneself from a manipulative family, but learning *how to avoid resorting to defensive maneuvers.* Defense and attack are complementary aspects of the same relational modality, which inevitably leads to sterile antagonism.

The many errors we have committed over the years, measured by our failure to reach the core of a family's dilemma, have convinced us of one thing—that the therapist, instead of reacting to one of the two levels on which the family relates to him, *must accept the family's entire "paradoxical" mechanism.* In this way, he will not need to defend himself from the family's contradictory responses because the family will be automatically deprived of its only means of contradicting him (Andolfi & Menghi, 1977). If the family fails to trap the therapist in this futile, paralyzing game, it will be on the spot and will be forced either to find other ways of relating or to break off the therapeutic relationship. In either case, a situation of uncertainty is created that may disrupt the stasis of the family system, which will now find it more difficult to change while standing still. Regardless of the type of intervention used, the therapist's strategy must remain firm, incorporating both of the contradictory levels of the family's request and making the therapeutic system operate at a higher level, where the contradictions can be comprehended and resolved.

As Selvini has brilliantly described in her paper "Why a Long Interval between Sessions?" (Selvini-Palazzoli, 1980), we have seen a marked change in the rhythm and duration of our current therapies in contrast with those of past years. Previously, therapies were often long (lasting several years) and the intervals between sessions were brief, because we thought that *the family could not make progress by itself.* We did not realize that we were actually reinforcing family stasis. Consequently, we created therapeutic systems in which the therapist became the guardian of everyone's emotional stability (including his own).

Today, the course of our therapies is very different because we define the relationships more rapidly. Whether or not the therapist succeeds in entering the system is determined within the first few sessions, or even in the first encounter. He may fail to enter into contact with major areas of the family, either because they are too well concealed or because at times the family may precipitously terminate the therapy even where the therapist has succeeded in touching vital conflicts and important contradictions. It is almost as if they feared the effects of a vital reawakening much more than their apparent psychological death.

The rapidity and intensity of our contact with the family increase the risk of sudden termination; however, this approach also makes it highly unlikely that the therapist will become enmeshed in an unproductive relationship. The sooner his redefinition occurs, the greater will be his incisiveness in the restructuring intervention. In some cases, the therapist may intentionally dwell at length on secondary details to confuse the family or distract attention from other therapeutic moves. In general, however, lingering over inessential elements while waiting for the "right moment" makes the therapist's moves more predictable, thus preventing tension from building. It appears to us that each system has a time limit within which a particular intervention has a chance to succeed. If this limit is passed without change having occurred, one must conclude that the family's ability to recognize and anticipate the pattern of the therapist's moves and to adjust their own responses to his moves are so adept as to annul any possible destabilizing effect.

We want to make clear that embracing the logic that imprisons the family and prevents the members from growing and individuating is not merely a technique, a method of using counterparadox in response to the paradox presented by the family. Rather, it is the result of the therapeutic choice in which the therapist determines how he intends to establish *his* relationship to the others. If he is able to accept the family's need to change and not to change, to request help and to refuse help, then the paradox presented by the family will probably become easier to understand. Its paradoxical dilemma will become a meeting ground instead of a phenomenon to judge or analyze with a microscope. By responding to both levels ("Yes, I will help you without changing you"), the therapist creates a strong bond with the family. The family will then perceive him as a person who can enter into its most intimate areas because he is able to neutralize the system's defenses without getting trapped in them.

If the therapist decides to work by observing the family's problems from "within," he will have to enter into the family's most obscure and hidden spaces. At the same time, he will need to distance himself from the family and return to his own space in every sequence of the therapeutic process. This engaging and disengaging, uniting and separating, that he uses as a model of relating requires him to be able to feel at once whole and divisible, to incorporate techniques and strategies without using them to avoid individuating himself in the therapeutic context (Minuchin & Fishman, 1981).

The Case of Tony: How to Identify Nodal Elements for an Alternative Structure

Tony is a young adult who was brought for therapy because of his catatonic symptomatology. His mother, who made the first contact by telephone, stated that her son had been behaving strangely for several months. He had not gone out of the house, had refused all contact with her and his siblings, and had withdrawn into complete mutism. He had had several psychiatric hospitalizations with no appreciable improvement. The mother presented the case as hopeless, but said she was confident that the therapist would be able to convince her son to return to normal.

The first session took place with the participation of Tony, his mother, his older brother, two sisters, and the five-year-old daughter of one of the sisters. Tony immediately took over the central role of identified patient. He paced slowly up and down the room, occasionally glancing wide-eyed at the other family members who huddled on a couch awaiting some resolutive response from the therapist.

The therapist, instead of sitting down and ignoring Tony's pacing, remained standing in a corner of the room, as though communicating to all present that only Tony had the right to decide when and how to begin the session. The therapist's behavior increased the tension already present in the context, transforming it into an interactional stress; instead of either enduring it or taking control over it, the therapist chose to participate in it. After a few minutes of silence that seemed full of mysterious significance, Tony decided to sit down, holding his body rigidly erect and tossing penetrating looks at the other family members who huddled even closer on the couch.

It was then the turn of the therapist, who sat down facing Tony. He finally broke the silence, addressing Tony's family in a firm voice: "I have a problem, and I don't think I can be of any help to you if you cannot first help me. I would like each of you to reassure me that you fully understand what Tony is saying to you." Then he invited each person, beginning with the mother, to find the best position from which to observe Tony and to listen carefully to everything that Tony wanted to say to him or her. Each member was asked to comply with this task without speaking.

What was the therapist trying to do by beginning this way? First of all, after transforming the tension that was initially directed at him alone by making it interactive, the therapist became even more unpredictable by presenting himself as the person with a problem and leaving it to the others to help him first (Andolfi & Angelo, 1981).

This is an example of what we have described as embracing the family's paradoxical logic and of responding simultaneously on two levels: We are willing to help (e.g., by actively participating in the encounter) without helping (that is, by redefining the family's expectations so radically that even the roles of help-seeker and help-giver are reversed).

If the therapist wants to avoid being trapped in a role by passively accepting the functions that others assign to him and participating in a drama with a foregone conclusion, then he must take part in the action. He has to redefine each player's role (including his own) and alter the timing and modality of each sequence, introducing new ways of playing the game.

In our experience we have found that the therapist can achieve this if he is able to promptly propose a different version of the family's script, changing it by amplifying the significance of the various functions. He will be effective as a director if the family group accepts him, and if, in the situation presented to him, he is able to differentiate the *nodal elements* on which to base his proposal for an alternative structure. These nodal elements exist in the contextual data most clearly indicative of the functional patterning of the system and of the relation that each member seeks to establish with the therapist. This exploration will not be easy because the family will reinforce its own definitions, insisting on the importance of more obvious and predictable data and indicating interconnections which deny any personal involvement (Andolfi & Angelo, 1981).

In the case of Tony, the boy's refusal to speak and the whole family's complicity concerning silence seemed to represent a focal element. Had the therapist addressed the boy, Tony's refusal to speak would have reinforced that horn of the family dilemma that needed the therapist to fail in order to prove that the situation was hopeless. If the therapist had spoken about Tony to the mother and siblings, he would have inevitably accentuated the division between the normal members (who speak) and the deviant member (who refuses to speak).

Instead, by asking the family members to help him precisely in that area where any initiative on his part was destined to fail, the therapist successfully thwarted any program the family might have had for the session. The therapist then implicitly redefined Tony's refusal to speak as another way of communicating something to the others. The other members were forced to abandon the role of passive, impotent spectators and to become cotherapists-protagonists in a situation that obliged them to differentiate themselves (instead of presenting themselves as a fused entity) and to expose themselves personally. By listening to Tony (who doesn't speak) and then reporting what they understood to the therapist, each person was forced to draw on and express his or her own fantasies and could not defend him/herself by giving stereotyped, impersonal information about Tony's behavior.

Asking the family members to collaborate by utilizing the system's defenses was a way of disrupting the rigid patterns that prevented each member from individuating and that kept Tony locked into the role of sentinel of the family fortress. And this would be exactly what the family wanted if it were not afraid of losing the security it had acquired by artificially dividing reality into separate parts. If the family members express resistance, saying it is impossible to communicate with Tony without using words, the therapist can insist that if Tony can speak with glances, then they must try harder to learn to do what Tony does so easily. In this way, the problem of refusing to speak is *reframed as a special ability*—to speak without words—that can be learned by the others as well. No one will refuse to try, because that would imply an explicit refusal to collaborate, which would be contrary to the real desire to change which is also present in the family system.

Once the context has been transformed in this way, even the identified patient no longer feels "free" to act out his refusal to speak because the therapist can ask him to do what he has asked the others to do: to *communicate without words* (that is, to engage in his symptomatic behavior—but at the therapist's request). Whether he speaks or refuses to speak, Tony will lose his function of controlling the family, which now perceives the therapist as an even greater threat to its stability.

In recomposing a mosaic, the addition of new fragments enables one to fit more pieces into place. Similarly, in the therapeutic scenario the individual family actors are encouraged to perform, utilizing parts of themselves which they had hoped to keep concealed, fearing their strong emotional implications. For this game of recomposition to take place, the therapist, too, has to risk exposure, utilizing his own fantasies in his relationship with the family. These fantasies, in which the elements supplied by the family are reintroduced in the form of images, actions, or scenes, stimulate the others to offer new information or to make further associations, in a circular process (Whitaker, 1975). An *intensification of the therapeutic relationship* occurs, as the nodal elements of the family script are brought together and reorganized by the therapist's suggestions, and he becomes an integral part of the new system.

As we can see from the case of Tony, the therapist immediately selects a *few* of the elements supplied by the family. These are magnified and made to serve as structural supports for an alternative script. Emphasis is placed on the *functions* of the various members, which are revealed through their nonverbal communications, such as posture, physical characteristics, the spatial positioning of the patient and of the others. The "historical" and "emotional" elements that have contributed to the definition of the respective functions are added gradually, as the therapist probes their significance in the developmental cycle of the family.

The family provides the "material," while the therapist places the trial markers for the course of associations.

THE THERAPIST AS DIRECTOR
OF THE FAMILY DRAMA

What counts are not the facts in themselves but their unfolding in each member's personal interpretation, the way in which each one links himself, his needs, his function within the family and the familial events perceived as most important along the continuum of the life-cycle (Andolfi & Angelo, 1981).

An illustration of this can be drawn from the first session with the family of Giorgio, a 26-year-old psychotic patient. Present besides the patient are: his 72-year-old father, who wears a hearing aid and sits at a considerable distance from the others, slumped over, giving the appearance of a man long dead whose position in the family has been taken over by his own ghost; his mother with a suffering expression, seated next to the patient, and an older brother and his wife who take the responsibility for relating the history of Giorgio's "illness." The brother's description emphasizes the organic aspect, tracing the origins to a cranial trauma caused by an automobile accident. He speaks with an air of competence, using a plethora of psychiatric terms ("delusional syndrome," "paranoid traits," etc.). He details the various diagnoses that have been made and the drugs that have been prescribed, continually asking the therapist which ones are most effective. A distinctly medical context is emerging, in which the symptoms discussed are seen as organically caused.

At this point the therapist interrupts the sequence by introducing a question to disrupt the script proposed by the family for this encounter. In trying to redefine the context, the language employed is of crucial importance. The therapist introduces a new language which translates and integrates the various nodal elements, pointing out interconnections that the family has not yet discerned and about which they are now forced to furnish new information. Once this occurs, the family has to become aware of this new input, thus laying the basis for change.

Therapist (*to Giorgio, who has been obtusely silent until now*): When did your father die, before or after you got sick?

Giorgio (*clearly perplexed, he stalls for time, asks for explanations; finally, sighing*): . . . Your question makes me feel uncomfortable really uncomfortable, yes, because . . . (*silence*). Excuse me, I have to go to the bathroom for a minute.

Mother: Yes, go ahead, you wanted to go even earlier.

Therapist: I think you can answer before you go.

Giorgio: Yes, I can say that . . . (*goes off the track*).

Therapist: Before or after?

Giorgio: Well, it happened after I got sick.

(*The same question is now posed to the other family members.*)

Brother: The truth is, I don't think he sees my father anymore as a person he can . . .

Therapist: But I'm not talking about Giorgio, I'm trying to find out how long your father has been dead.

(*The mother interrupts; she hasn't been able to stand it these last four years, the worries . . .*)

Brother: For about a year, I'd say, ever since he completely lost his hearing.
Therapist Later, then?
Brother: Yes, yes.
Mother: After (*silence*).
Therapist: Did he die of heartbreak?
Mother: Well, well, sure . . . after, you see, a little bit at a time.
Therapist: So now you have a new head of the family?
Mother: That's just it, we don't know what to do. We have to find the right medicine. (*She continues talking about how hard it is for her to bear the situation.*)
Therapist: (*He takes out a prescription pad and leans toward the mother, as though intending to comply with her request to prescribe effective medication.*) If I am to prescribe the right medication, you will have to help me understand whether it should be medicine for a crazy guy who suddenly had to take over his father's place, or medicine for a crazy guy who purposely killed his father so he could take his place. I think that's the problem, and we can't continue until we get an answer.

It becomes clear here that the language utilized by the therapist is of fundamental importance. Through its judicious use he has been able to integrate certain nodal elements, finding connections which the family has not yet established but with which it is now forced to deal. As the family participates in this process it must accept the therapist into its system, thereby laying the foundation for change.

Just what is it that enables him to grasp the distribution and characteristics of the reciprocal functions rapidly? In the first contact and during the course of the first session, the family members supply many elements through their verbal and nonverbal communications and through interactional redundancies. These elements are perceived by the therapist in the form of a comprehensive gestalt on which he bases his effort to redefine the situation. In the case cited above, he noticed the father's posture and spatial position, the older brother's behavior, the mother's position next to the patient and her blank expression, and the fact that she sat between her two sons. These elements all seemed to indicate that the father had long lost his position in the family and that his two sons had been delegated to take over for him, one with the function of "the wise one"; the other of "the crazy one." The therapist actively organizes the elements supplied by the family to construct a new framework which will be gradually built upon during the course of the session as new information emerges.

In other words, the material that the family presents contains certain elements that are particularly significant and pertinent to any redefinition of the existing relations among the family members. These elements, which we describe as "nodal," represent points of intersection of the different and mutually exclusive scripts proposed respectively by the family and the therapist as frameworks for ordering the family's history.

This concept is illustrated in Figure 3. Diagrams of two different suits of clothing are represented in a limited space which they in part share. Imagine that the outer circle enclosing the diagrams contain all

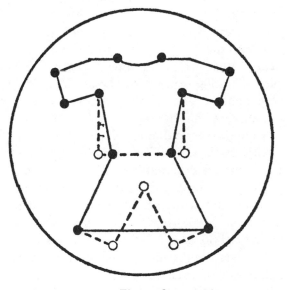

Figure 3

of the available information concerning the family's history. If we suppose that the model proposed by the family corresponds to the "dress" outlined by the black dots and continuous lines, then the model constructed by the therapist corresponds to the "shirt and pants" represented by the same black dots plus the white dots and the broken lines. With the introduction of a few "nodal" points we can draw new outlines which change the gestalt and the overall significance of the image.

The family will try to impose its own "suit of clothes," describing it in minute detail and inviting the therapist to share its own frame of reference. If he lets himself become enmeshed in this operation, the therapist risks accepting the family's model as his own. In the case of Giorgio, if the therapist had allowed the family to continue at length describing all of the patient's past medical and psychiatric history, he would have automatically reinforced the family's image of the patient and of the correlated functions of the other members. Therefore it becomes crucial that he quickly gather in all of the significant elements which surface, reorganizing them into an alternative script. With the success of this move he takes control of the therapeutic process. He also creates an unanticipated imbalance in the rigid definition of each one's assigned function which interferes with the family's attempts at homeostatic compensation.

The analysis presented here can easily give rise to misunderstandings. For example, it may seem as though the therapist is trying to impose on the family an arbitrary framework that is "extraneous" to the family's problems. Similar doubts may be reinforced by the therapist's extremely active behavior, which may at times seem "manipulative." However, it is our view that the therapist does not introduce "extraneous" elements into the script that is being dramatized by the family in its encounter with the therapist. Everything the therapist says or does during the session is based on material that emerges from the transactions. He merely *restructures* the elements that are offered (Menghi, 1977): emphasizing some which have previously gone unnoticed; relegating others that had been overemphasized to the background, or altering their sequential positions. He proposes an alternative structure by introducing isolated and vaguely defined images which stimulate the family to elaborate on them further. These images serve as a skeletal structure for the family to build on, which takes form gradually only as new information is added. By information we mean not static historical data but information concerning interactive patterns.

On the other hand, utilizing the data in the family history enables the therapist to create a strong bond with the family, and this is a prerequisite for the continuation of therapy. Certain interventions which seem totally arbitrary and interrupt interactive sequences in reality serve to translate on a verbal level what the therapist has perceived nonverbally or through his own associations. The organization of the material is clearly the result of an active process on the part of the therapist and is influenced by his personal history and personality. In this sense, we can say that the therapist and his perceptive power are the "extraneous elements" that are introduced into the system. If we ask what it is that the therapist is trying to achieve, the immediate answer is: to change the family's rules.

If the therapy is successful, the family's original functional rigidity gradually gives way to increased elasticity in the attribution of individual functions. The initial, highly stabilized family structure is gradually replaced by a new organization, the therapeutic one which is *unstable* and *provisory*. The process is complete when the family members have learned to make their own choices, free of rigid models, when they have developed the capacity to accept the "unpredictable," when the unexpected itself forms a part of their "rules" (Andolfi & Angelo, 1981).

To accomplish this they must learn and learn again the ways to modify their former blueprints for elaborating experience. An event of this magnitude justifies the resistance which the family brings into play. Now the principal problem becomes how to overcome this resistance. The method presented in this book is one possible response.

CHAPTER 3

Redefinition as the Matrix of Change

REDEFINING THE THERAPEUTIC RELATIONSHIP

As was evident in the preceding chapter, the formation of a therapeutic system demands continuous redefinition or reframing on the part of the therapist. He begins with the more or less explicit definition which the family presents of itself and then he attempts to modify this, changing the significance of the familial interaction or the interaction between the family members and himself. The goal of this is to disturb the patterns of interaction among the various subsystems in order to render them untenable and to create stable changes and supportive values in the relational scheme.

Given the remarkable ability of these families to assimilate all new learning into their usual patterns, every redefinition risks being engulfed within the old, known patterns and thus rendered inoperable.

The family then will try to impose its own rules in the therapeutic system, seeking to draw the therapist into their "game." From the first session the therapist must recognize the necessity of reframing the relationships within the family subsystem and between himself and one or more members of the family. Change in even one relationship has consequences affecting the others, since all contribute to the equilibrium of the system. In fact, whatever significant stimulus is introduced into the system will tend to change the relationship among family members because it draws forth new elements and responses. But if the therapist observes that his new input is used to recreate the same old rigid balance under a new guise, he must change the redefinition or amplify the complexity in such a way as to maintain the imbalance (uncertainty) which will permit the relationship to evolve (Whitaker, 1975). If the organizing of all new information into the old patterns is to be avoided, the understanding of the relationships demands recognition of changing and changeable definitions.

The family employs explicit and implicit modalities in defining itself. All the attitudes and nonverbal behaviors which color interaction within the family, as well as between family members and the therapist, contribute to these modalities. The therapist, in turn, may redefine the relationship at both the explicit (mainly verbal) and the implicit (mainly nonverbal) levels, as we see in the following portion of a therapy session.

The family in therapy is composed of a 14-year-old psychotic boy, his father and mother, and an older brother who was not present at this first session. From the very beginning the patient focuses attention upon himself through the use of bizarre behavior and inappropriate language, causing his parents to react with embarrassment and anxiety.

Therapist: For how long does he make you listen to this "music" each day?
Father: All the time.
Therapist: How many hours more or less (*turning to patient*)?
Carlo: It depends on them, on how much they bother me.
Therapist: So if they nag you too much you respond with the "music"?
Carlo: Well, it's a matter of your point of view. When they have to talk to yours truly they say, "You always exaggerate, always the same

things, you're fixated." But who goes to paradise? . . . Those
who are fixated!

Father: What's that supposed to mean?

Carlo: Well in paradise . . . justice, truth, . . . do you people know
where you stand?

Therapist (*casually, apparently not listening, takes an ashtray and extends it toward the patient*): Could you hold this a moment while
I speak?

Carlo: With pleasure! (*He takes the ashtray and holds it up in one hand
disconcertedly, consequently appearing somewhat ridiculous
and absurd.*)

Therapist: But hold it in a standing position, like this . . . (*he slightly
alters the position of the patient, causing him to appear even more
unnatural*).

Therapist (*turning to the parents*): Which of you thinks of this boy
more as an eccentric or more as a crazy man? Which of the two
descriptions?

Father: Well, we know he's . . . .

Therapist: No, just give me a simple answer.

Father: Um, half and half, because we hope that it's a passing thing.
Because before he was fine. Two years ago he was as normal as
anybody.

Therapist: Yes, but today . . . ?

Father: Well, we think about the same.

Mother: Perhaps he's more optimistic.

Therapist: What does optimism signify? Is it more toward craziness or
more toward eccentricity?

Father: Seeing him as eccentric, without a doubt.

As one sees, the therapist's redefinition not only makes the patient's
behavior seem ridiculous and dispels the climate of anxiety and drama
surrounding the family, but also creates a context within which his actions appear rational, connoting that his bizarre behavior is voluntary
and has a precise meaning. At the same time the patient gets the indirect message: "If you want to establish a useful rapport with me, you've
got to give more, discussing your problems comprehensibly without
using infantile tricks. You've been successful in fooling your parents,

but don't think you can do the same with me." At the same time the parents get the implicit message not to be taken in and to try to look at their son somewhat differently.

Even if the therapist's request for information other than what the family members are giving him seems directed solely at focusing on a specific problem or behavior, in reality it is directed at seeing this behavior in relation to the behavior of the others. Through the questions that arise in a relational "syntax," the differences in behavior of the various members of the family system acquire important informational value (Selvini-Palazzoli, 1980). This way of gathering information then becomes an attempt at reframing.

The exchange described, as opposed to other techniques, does not strive to make the family members communicate in a more comprehensible way. Communication is always mediated through the therapist, who selects and introduces the "input" through the questions he poses. We wouldn't consider a confrontation or even a dialogue among the members at a session so necessary were it not for the fact that it gives the therapist the raw material for his interventions; the most useful exchanges may, in fact, occur spontaneously outside of the therapy session through elaboration and definition of that which took place during the session. Change takes place through each member's continuous work in attempting to define himself in respect to the definition offered by the therapist, which should bring about changes in the values being played upon and in the patterns of the relationship. This is designed to modify and amplify the distribution of personal space and to liberate all the energy heretofore dedicated to stereotypical interactive functions.

REDEFINITION OF THE CONTEXT

We define ourselves not only through our words but also through our actions, through the instruments, objects and means we choose, the manner in which we use them, and what they signify to us. All of these components create the context of our interactions and exchanges and are, in turn, conditioned by those same exchanges.

In therapy, too, one must notice behaviors involving the use of personal or shared objects, ritual acts, etc. These are used to qualify intentions, comment on the behavior of others, and, taken together, develop the context within which relational exchanges may take place. Sometimes it suffices to introduce a new element, such as using a new movement, having someone change his place, altering the rhythm of the interactions by imposing silence or suggesting exchanges between certain members of the family system (Andolfi, 1979; Selvini-Palazzoli, 1970). This change of context will, in turn, alter successive transactions. Acting on the elements and using them, the therapist can then redefine the relations at many levels, as seen in the following.

Participants in this session are a 20-year-old anorectic patient, her parents, and a younger sister. The context appears falsely cooperative. The family uses an "interpretive style" learned in the course of a preceding therapeutic experience and the atmosphere created is one of total stagnation. The mother appears the most committed to this activity, as she controls the scene so that no very intense emotions emerge. Halfway through the session the therapist starts fooling with an ashtray beside him, picks up some cigarette butts and begins slowly and methodically (with a distracted air while not speaking) to let the tobacco fall to the floor. The family continues speaking but each member observes fascinatedly for longer and longer periods until there is a heavy silence.

Therapist (*turned toward the mother but continuing his "work" with the cigarette butts*): Why not try to do what I'm doing? If you did, you might be able to listen instead of being caught in the sea of words you've all been drowning in for so many years. (*He gives her a cigarette butt which she automatically starts to tear open.*)

Mother (*after a long silence*): I'm tearing up everything. Is that what you mean?

Therapist: That's what I would think if I put myself in your place.

Mother: That's right. Everything is coming apart. Everything I say is useless, or mistaken. Maybe unconsciously I only think about myself and not the others. I may be on the wrong track. I just don't know . . .

Therapist: Well, why not try to find the "butts" which belong to mother, which to father, and which to the daughters?

Mother: Exactly—it's total confusion.

Therapist: Instead of talking why not take apart another cigarette butt (*offering her others in the palm of his hand*).
Mother: So what can these people do beyond ask for help?
Therapist: They can take part . . .
Mother: At a certain point that finishes . . .
Therapist: No, there are lots of cigarette butts around — you see them everywhere. Some people break them up with their hands, some who do it with their minds, always breaking up the remains of things. There are some who transfer everything to the cerebral level (*indicating the anorectic patient and referring to her "intellectualizing"*) to the point of eating cerebrally, urinating cerebrally, defecating cerebrally, and to even cerebrally lick the crumbs of others' lives.

The context of the session is slowly modified through nonverbal behavior and the ongoing exchange takes on other significance. The cigarette butt used by the therapist and the slow rhythm of his crumbling of it point up the useless verbosity of the family in a temporal dimension and underscore the atmosphere of deadly boredom which it creates. At the moment when one might expect the therapist to pay close attention to the attempts of the family to appear convincing and cooperative, he removes himself from what is happening and becomes involved in a seemingly irrelevant action completely unrelated to the preceding context. It is as if he were saying nonverbally, "Nothing you are saying interests me because I know that what you say doesn't correspond to your real feelings and, above all, not to what concerns you most right now. Your words show that each of you has lost faith in your ability to have a satisfying relationship with the others. Only if you can accept living and feeling your sense of impotence can you hope to draw forth something useful from this therapy."

The new context redefines not only the internal relationships of the family, demystifying their verbal exchanges, but also the relationship between the family and the therapist. The latter initially uses a marginal involvement to remain outside of the primary context, in order to create a different context in which his position is more central and of greater weight.

As in other types of redefinition, the redefinition of the context demonstrates that the more effective interventions are tied to the implicit level where, for the most part, nonverbal communication is utilized. This level is less manipulable and less likely to engender defensive responses.

REDEFINITION OF THE PROBLEM

The redefinition of the problem presented by the family with its request for therapy is possible if one succeeds in changing the significance attributed to the symptomatic behavior of the patient. This is not possible to do until the family system is artificially removed from its habitual context, where all the old "natural" patterns are intertwined. It is as if one confounded a crystal with the chemical elements of which it is composed, seeing only *one* of the possible structural expressions. Our objective, therefore, is to transfer the symptom to the relational plane, doing so in such a way that it becomes clear to all that it functions to maintain the rapport of the family. It becomes necessary to analyze the structure of that which the problem is a manifestation and to redefine the relationships which cause it. If we succeed in removing the reductive and undervaluing labels and attitudes generally directed toward the "disturbed one," we can then hope to connect the patient in alternative relational dimensions. From this new point of departure, new ways of relating may be sought. The symptomatic behavior which is habitually seen as an individual problem must become the problem of all family members *in a more complex reality.* This must not be done by explaining the concept of circularity to the family, as is sometimes done, but rather by redefining, in practice, the relationships and the context within which all takes place. This means that, together with the family, one must separate and restructure the elements which constitute the problem and then arrange them in a different dimension.

As an example let us look at part of the first session with the family of a 12-year-old girl, Laura, sent to us for problems of "depression and anorexia." Since the moment that the earliest disturbances were perceived, the family has lived more or less separated. Following the advice of a psychologist, Laura and her mother moved in with relatives. Since then Laura has demanded that her parents take turns staying at her side. At this session Laura is present with her parents and her sisters, nine-year-old Marina and five-year-old Carla. Early in the session we had spoken of the importance of the maternal grandmother, who reportedly had a very "sweet" way of treating Laura. Laura, however, denies that this is so.

Mother (*to Laura*): Can I tell the doctor that before you got sick you were very close to your grandmother?

Laura: Yes. Yes.

Therapist (*to the mother*): Excuse me, but do you always ask your daughter's permission when you want to say what you think?

Mother: Before, I never asked anyone's permission. Now, with this situation at home, for fear of hurting her feelings . . .

Laura (*interrupting*): Anyway, you've already told him!

Mother: . . . I ask her permission.

Therapist: Do you ask anyone else for permission when you want to give your own opinion about something?

Mother: No, no one else . . . not my husband.

Laura: No, now you ask everyone.

Mother: Well, maybe now I do ask everyone for permission because I feel a little like a person who's under accusation, if you know what I mean.

Therapist: You feel like that?

Mother: Yes, that's just how I feel. I think twice before I open my mouth because I always think I'm making a mistake.

Therapist: That's a bad state to be in! . . . (*turning to the father*) Does father also ask Laura's permission when he wants to say something?

Father: Normally, no . . . not even now. Perhaps I'm mistaken, but I sometimes say what I think. (*to Laura*) Isn't that true?

Therapist (*to the wife*): You know, it seems to me that your husband follows your lead very well.

Mother: You mean my husband does what I do?

Therapist: About asking permission, he does just what you do.

Mother: It depends on how you're looking at it.

Therapist (*to Laura*): Move your chair over here, about halfway between your Mother and Dad. (*Laura moves over and sits down between her parents.*)

Mother: Well, right now I guess he really does.

Therapist (*to Laura in a serious voice*): Laura, are you a 12-year-old girl or a King Kong?

Laura: A 12-year-old girl.

Therapist (*to Laura*): Then why do they treat you at home as if you were King Kong? Do you know who King Kong is?

Laura: Yes, sure.

Therapist (*to younger sisters*): Do you know who King Kong is? (*replying to their negative nodding*) Well, then, Laura—you explain it to them.

Laura: He's an enormous, very strong ape; they even made a movie about him.

(*The therapist leaves the room and returns with a pile of cushions which he puts on Laura's chair to raise her higher. Now she is positioned between her parents but higher.*)

Therapist: You see! I don't mean that you are like a big ape but that you are like a very tall person who is above everyone else and of whom everyone else is a bit afraid. Have you noticed how your mother and father watch you when you speak? Listen, how did you do it? When I was 12, I wasn't so important in my home as you are. What's your secret? How did you become so important?

Laura (*from her raised position, angrily*): I'm not important, not even now. I'm just normal.

Therapist (*to Laura*): Do your parents ask permission more often from you or from your grandmother?

Laura: Let's see . . . not from either one of us.

Therapist: What do you mean? Didn't you hear your mother say that she's afraid of making a mistake everytime she opens her mouth and that makes her always feel embarrassed?

Laura: Well, I don't believe it.

Therapist (*to mother*): You see, not only do you feel awkward but they don't even believe you!

Mother: That's exactly the way it is!

Therapist (*to father*): Do you believe your wife has been in difficulty lately?

Father: Yes, I really think she has.

Laura (*in a resentful tone*): Hm, hm, hm!

Therapist: I've listened carefully to all your arrangements, but, frankly, I'd like you to help me understand what it is we can work on together because the matter still isn't clear to me.

As is evident, the problem as accepted within the family is redefined through a different interpretation of the stated relationships and of the roles attributed to the persons involved. The figure of Laura, described above as a depressed and passive child in great need of help and love, through the questions acquires a totally different connotation, drastically changing her role. Observing the relationships among father, mother, and child, it becomes clear that the respective positions of power in the family are reversed: The "poor child" bedeviled by her illness becomes the center of power. It is she who exercises the greatest control over intrafamilial communication. This has been acquiesced to and ceded to her, based on the needs of the whole family. To reinforce the "new" image of Laura, the therapist first uses a spatial rearrangement, which vividly structures the relationship between Laura and her parents; then, in using the cushions he brings into focus the absurdity of her role.

In the session there is a progressive changing of the context, with the discussion of the family relationships approaching the grotesque with the reference to King Kong. Anxiety builds higher and higher, only to then expend itself in liberating laughter.

It is clear that the subdivisions of the various types of redefinition which we have discussed are useful as teaching tools. In application, explicit, implicit, and contextual redefinitions are almost always used simultaneously and one reinforces the other. The explicit redefinition is set up, modulated, and clarified by the implicit, and vice versa. The context is changed by the verbal and nonverbal redefinitions and it, in turn, may render these more effective or absolutely useless.

CHAPTER 4

Provocation as a Therapeutic Intervention

INDUCING A CRISIS

In rigid families, the suspicion that someone may threaten their usual interactive schemes, removing himself from the rules of the game, leads each member to more closely check on the others and brings about strong emotional tension. In daily life, each member of these families chooses not to choose, compelled by anxiety and tension to always act in such a way as to appear under the banner of a crystallized myth of unity (Ferreira, 1963). The tension functions as fuel for the ongoing labor of transforming much in order to guarantee that nothing really changes.

But if, on one hand, the tension works toward maintaining homeostasis, on the other hand its intensity may in time reach a level sufficiently high as to thrust toward change. This does not mean that when these families decide to seek therapy they are disposed to question their own rules, but rather that the internal tension has reached a point which can no longer be contained through the function served by the identified patient. That is, the identified patient cannot guarantee that the habitual interactional scheme can be maintained. The presence of a patient notwithstanding, the fears of unbalancing their equilibrium, with the concomitant possibilities of having to renegotiate rules, each one's functions, and defined space, increase again. The danger of uncontrolled change in each one's status looms up again.

The symptomatology of the identified patient represents the two instances in which the family takes action in seeking therapy. In one instance it is a request for help; in the other it is fear of a crisis. Indeed, it is the fear of the instability essential to reaching a new balance of unity and differentiation which has already pushed the family members into their rigid, no-longer-adequate modes of interaction. In the past the threat of a crisis gave rise to interactive patterns already worn out and ineffective; now facing the need for therapy, the family, more than ever, will feel itself threatened and united in the attempt to avoid a crisis as much wished for as feared.

The therapeutic intervention, therefore, may be seen from two different angles—one being the very real suffering involved and the other being the internal logic of the family's functioning. If, in order to maintain their unvarying pattern, the family finds that the use of the scapegoat is no longer sufficient, it becomes necessary to bring in new elements. To effect this, the family members use an old ploy; since family rigidity does not permit the discovery of new schemes, they focus on one person—someone outside of the nuclear family—with the goal of having him absorb all their tensions. With a mechanism similar to that used with the patient, they are capable of transferring their tensions and drawing the outsider into the logic "help us because we no longer know how to."

Often these families have successfully searched out among family and friends persons suited to helping them while reinforcing the old family structure. But frequently, when the going gets tough, these improvised therapists precipitously bow out. This becomes the moment when the need is felt for a "real professional"—someone who doesn't leave you in the lurch, someone who knows how to treat the mentally ill. It becomes clear that the presence of the therapist allows the family

to put into motion a mechanism analogous to that used with the identified patient, i.e., to shunt to him all of the tension which can no longer
be contained. The therapist will be expected to manage that tension in
such a way as to leave their established "order" untouched, and most
importantly, not to undermine their definition of the illness of the patient. They will ask that the therapist enter into their logic, seeing the
patient as the only source of difficulty. If he lends himself to this, he
will find himself with the same burden as the identified patient: that of
being cut off from the others in the system.

The designation of the patient and the request for therapy come at
different times but they may be considered analogous in their functional significance. In both instances the family seeks to avoid tension
among its member by electing an official "carrier" of these tensions.
And in both instances, just because it sees itself as threatened, the entire family will more than ever struggle to sustain its dysfunctional
structure. Paradoxically, it must appear stronger when it actually feels
weaker. It must be realized not only that the family is more rigid than
usual at the moment that it asks for therapy, but also that the request
for therapy is implicitly an interactive modality for transferring this
rigidity into the new therapeutic system. Even if the symptomatology
of the patient is the most apparent signal in triggering the confrontation with their own suffering, it is the very real terror of doing this which
would tempt the therapist to put band-aids on the deep wounds which
have opened up within their organization. The hidden agenda, the
principal exigency in seeking therapy, is to maintain distance from a
crisis which appears threatening and uncontrollable.

Jackson and other therapists have already noted how relatively useless are attempts to provoke rapid changes in families which are not in
crisis, and how sometimes it is much more effective to proceed in such
a way that "the family system leaves its self-imposed limits" (Jackson,
1957). Haley (1971) has also underlined the importance of interview-
ing families when they are off balance, indicating how much more difficult it is to change their organization if treatment has already brought
some relief to the problem. Hoffman (1981) supports this further
when she states that often therapy cannot bring back order; rather, it
must introduce complexity. In other words, to a family system which

asks for help in resolving its difficulties but wants merely to circumscribe them, it is fitting to give a response which increases the variables in play to the point of triggering a loss of control over the preexisting equilibrium.

Clinical experience has taught us to reinforce these observations. If we truly wish to activate improvement there must, of necessity, be a state of crisis in the functioning of the family. Our role, therefore, becomes the opposite of that which the family expects, because we seek to induce that very imbalance which it seeks to avoid. Not only must our interpretation of their discomfort be much broader than theirs, but also their wounds must be redefined by our intervention. Where an instability exists it will be our goal to accentuate it. Where none is obvious we must work to bring it to the surface. The family asks for stability and we induce greater instability: a "blow-out" in place of a patch.

The possibility of exposing a crisis in the family is strictly related to the intensity of the intervention. How many times in the past we have tried to move a mountain with a pick and shovel! Looking back at some of our therapy we have seemed rather pathetic in those attempts to "respect the family and its time," without being aware of the distortion between our noble intentions and the rapidity with which the family neutralized our every move.

An anorectic patient of 18 speaks monotonously about how she suffers, feeling herself cut in two, one part which wants to grow and one which wants to remain a child. If we had not observed the absolute control the girl exerts over her parents and siblings and how little they do to frustrate her, we might feel touched by her dilemma. Feeling it necessary, however, to learn more about this situation, we pose other questions to her and the family. If we had not observed the evident incongruity between the gravity of the symptomatology of the girl and the intellectual, "salon" tone of the family, we might have waited for each one to express his or her ideas on the subject in the hope that eventually some discord would surface. We might have let the girl pour out everything in the hope that she would finally say something which could result in a real conflict. Whoever has worked with these families knows only too well that this would never happen, but that one might enter into an inescapable labyrinth, where each person demonstrates his or her satisfaction at being an expert involved in such interesting material, but where no one takes a risk at unearthing a more scorching level.

Our patient would have continued to feel well protected within that family mechanism which, in exchange for her refusal to live normally, offers her the possibility of never making autonomous choices while always occupying center stage. The parents would have continued to avoid any confrontation and younger sister would have deluded herself in thinking that she could ever be free of the shadow of the sick sister. All this would have been possible with the help and support of a "respecting" therapist.

During the past several years we have come to realize that the family feels sustained, above all, by the intensity of the therapeutic impact. It is truly in experiencing the ability of the therapist and his capacity to rapidly take control of the therapeutic relationship, breaking with the habitual interactive patterns of the family, that they feel support and containment. In fact, if it is true that in the struggle for control of the relationship the family does not give up its weapons easily, it is also true in this skirmish that it will gain from the therapist's security in not letting himself be trapped in their schema. Consequently, they may better accept the risks of a change with his guidance.

But if our first objective is to induce a therapeutic crisis, we must be certain we have the strength to provoke one and to do it in such a manner that the intensity of the crisis is directly in proportion to the degree of rigidity present in the family system. Our intervention is posited, therefore, as a response to the messages sent us by the family from the initial steps of the relationship which they seek to establish with us. The mechanics of setting up a meeting, the telephone calls prior to the first session, the manipulation involving the presence or absence of family members, the first minutes of the first encounter—all give us an idea of the possibilities for being absorbed into the family's rules. The intensity of the intervention is rooted in our vulnerability, which is obviously subjective and bound to the unique rapport established between *that therapist* and *that family*.

Observing the intensity and quality of the communications directed our way by the family, we have learned to respond almost mimetically. That is, we imitate certain messages, accentuating their intensity in proportion to that intensity which we have received. If the intensity of the intervention is in direct proportion to the rigidity of the family system, the quality of our response mirrors that same intensity in response to the communications received from the family. A careful reading of these allows us to evaluate those messages which would pose the greatest difficulty to us and to "restore" to the family those messages which do not antagonize them on those planes, but which faithfully shore up their structure.

Experience has taught us that it is futile to argue with the family about who is right. Our strategy is to affirm that the family, with all of its incongruous messages, is always right. In this way, we force the family to experience the pain of its own contradictions. At this point the family members themselves will be able to see a real change in their relations with each other as less threatening and possibly more liberating.

THE IDENTIFIED PATIENT: THE ENTRANCE INTO THE SYSTEM

The symptomatic behavior, usually considered an expression of the suffering of the individual and other members of the family system, undoubtedly presents advantages for both. We often commit the error of undervaluing the enormous power connected to the function of the scapegoat. The involuntary quality of the symptom, in fact, permits the "patient" to define and control his relationships with the others, as well as to control the relationships among the other family members. Consequently, the great accord which usually covers all the differences within these families is that the sick one, the person to be cured, is solely he—the identified patient. The fact is that he functions as the homeostatic regulator of every family transaction and that because of his "illness" all the family relationships of reciprocal function-dependence which chain one to the other may crystallize over time and make his presence essential to all of them. With this understanding, the impossibility of interrupting the relentless control which each one exercises over the other takes on a justification which is more than plausible.

The enormous importance of the function of the scapegoat explains why all attempts at displacing his centrality and broadening the problem to embrace all of the family relationships are so difficult and usually destined to fail. To accept a redefinition of this "arrangement" signifies to the family that, in fact, it will lose its most effective instrument for maintaining its habitual circuit. It signifies confronting, all too precipitously, the poverty of their interactions, the closed-off quality of any real exchanges, and the almost nonexistent personal space left to each member. In practice, such attempts usually result in the family's leaving therapy or entering into an interminable and useless polemic with the therapist.

In support of this we must note that the identified patient is very often "brought" into therapy. In fact, since he is the patient, no one grants him any power of decision, nor does he ask for it. Even if he is the one to seek the intervention and acts as the central element in gathering the family together, he is permitted this only in his role of being "different." In therapeutic sessions his behavior appears to reinforce at least five basic elements which the entire family displays in therapy:

1) The absolute *centrality* of his function as the "sick one," which by now fills the world of the family, blocking out every other problem. He is no longer a person but rather an illness; all the others have become doctors and nurses.
2) The illogic of his communications, even the most banal and seemingly adequate.
3) The *involuntary quality of all "his" behavior* so that all of the patient's actions are accepted with sad resignation: "It isn't he who is doing this, it's his illness." All of the family shares this thought, and taking his cue, the identified patient may allow himself any and all types of behaviors.
4) The *harmful consequences* which the identified patient's illness brings to the entire family; i.e. "If we didn't have this cross to bear, ours would be a truly happy family."
5) The *uselessness of effort* exerted by everyone—family, friends, and doctors—in changing the patient's behavior. It is implicit in this manifestation of good faith which didn't pay off that no one must ever be better than those who have already tried to help.

Based upon this edifice, the family system makes its request: "Help us to change the patient without interfering with our relationships. Help us to help him recover even if it is impossible."

Not long ago the mother of a schizophrenic patient called our institute to ask about starting in therapy. She spoke to our secretary with such urgency that our secretary felt obliged to interrupt a session so that one of our therapists could speak with her immediately. She asked for an appointment at once, stating at the same time that the situation had dragged on unchanged over the past 11 years. She also added that she had consulted so many therapists and so many clinics that she didn't any longer believe that her son could recover. She said that she hoped, in fact, that the doctor wouldn't start searching through her relationship with her son, that it had already been tried in Switzerland and nothing at all resulted from it. She concluded by saying that there, at least, they were "human," whereas in Italy she had been the victim of incredible cynicism. Asked if her son had participated in the decision to undertake a new therapy, she responded that in any case he never responds verbally and that probably if she had asked him he would have said no and, further, that he could even have behaved violently toward her.

Not to see the incongruity between an apparent request for change and a real request for immutability, between a request for recovery and a more or less explicit definition of the impossibility of recovery, means invariably that one falls into the homeostatic game which maintains the identified patient in his function as the "ill one." How is it possible to cure someone who is defined as incurable? How is it possible to cure the patient if it is impossible to change the rules which support his behavior? Anytime that we have accepted an open therapeutic role dealing with the mixed messages being communicated to us, sooner or later the hopelessness of curing the patient and the normality of the family have become points of contention: The therapist is committed to move the family toward real change, while the family is set to demonstrate its magnanimous good will and the failure of the therapist.

The tension and aggressivity which these situations usually generate in the therapist move us to linger over a rather obvious fact: Within the communications received from these families are *elements which are highly provocative.*

If we examine the sequencing in the preceding example we can see how the therapist might feel extremely provoked, especially in his role. The patient's mother asks for the help of an expert, at the same time denying him the attributes which his specialization connotes. In substance she asks to be helped because she feels impotent, but it is she, nevertheless, who defines the time and the method of the intervention. The eventuality of the spontaneous initiative of the therapist is foreseen as useless " . . . nothing can come of it . . . ," or dangerous, " . . . he might have even become violent. . . . " Posing an urgent problem, she exerts emotional pressure on the therapist to whom she communicates; however, she stresses the uselessness of prompt participation in therapy considering the chronic quality of the situation. Soon after she insinuates that the therapist may be cynical, " . . . at least in Switzerland they were human . . . here in Italy, on the other hand . . . " — all of this supports her true lack of faith in the possible success of a therapy so sought after.

After observing the provocative messages sent by the families, we formulated an early hypothesis for working with them. Why not focus on the provocative aspects of the communications coming from these families and imagine the strategic interventions which would be their responses?

Originally that hypothesis was not fully examined, nor did we strain to develop it into a real theory. It represented, however, a point of departure for a series of initiatives. We decided to select some communications from the family and to respond in such a way as to emphasize certain components. Thus we could relegate much information to a secondary position, emphasizing other communications, above all those which struck us as provocative. This required our separating the entire complex of the family's communicative mode into many parts, of which only some, those most intensely provocative, would be used. Instead of resorting to challenging or antagonizing the family, the therapist would make use of the very components which might have drawn him into unproductive positions. Our analysis of the aforementioned telephone call is an example of "reading" the message in this way. In fact, we selected only the elements considered provocative. All the other messages — and the call was full of them — were set aside. As these messages were chosen by the therapist, they became the ongoing structure of a new interaction between him and the mother.

From the moment that the provocation of certain familial communication is perceivable and valuable in an absolutely subjective way, any therapist may respond to the family by personally joining it (Menghi, 1977). As the fruit of a new and intense relationship between "therapist" and "family," a fresh communicative pattern may grow, in which the therapist, while being an integral part of the system, is, at the same time, in control.

We hypothesized that our counterprovocative response might use the identified patient as the point of attack in the system: *If the family provokes the therapist and controls the therapeutic system through the identified patient, the therapist, too, must try to provoke the family and to control the therapeutic system using the same channel.* Instead of opposing the centrality of the identified patient, we sought to use it. We thought that an effective way to enter these family systems might be to accentuate and maintain the position of the scapegoat. This would be our *point of entry into the system.* If the system itself had chosen him to carry the burden of the family problems and to mediate every interaction, then we would do likewise, nailing him to his function. His behavior, defined as involuntary, would have to come to be seen as absolutely voluntary in the eyes of the family. The identified patient, by definition the central figure because of his inability to behave adequately and autonomously, would have to be openly challenged by the therapist, who would affirm his centrality while making him appear, however, completely intentional in his behavior.

In this way the perception of the problem and the therapist-family relationship would be radically redefined by an intense and disorienting provocation to the entire family system. The redefinition then becomes an integrating element and the final outcome of the provocation.

Marco is 16. For some months he has been speaking strangely, saying he is an Indian and taking on Indian-like attitudes. At school he is increasingly isolated. Often, when he hears certain words, he taps his ears and, crying, heaps invective upon his father and mother. On the telephone, mother reports that she is helpless in the face of this. She appears extremely worried, but at the same time she seems to participate viscerally in her son's behavior. She goes on in the greatest detail to describe the eccentricities, the gestures, and the language of his "Apache" state. The therapist is struck by the contradictory attitudes coming from the mother: on one hand her great worry about her son, and on the other hand the vivacity and familiarity with which she enters into his "Indian story." The monotony with which she furnishes information about their family life contrasts openly with the vitality exhibited when discussing Marco's symptoms. To the therapist the mother's message sounds more or less like this: "Marco and his Indian business are the only points of interest in my life; help me to change his actions." There is no need for further comment on the problem posed for the therapist.

At this point one might conjecture and hypothesize about the relational significance of the information gathered over the telephone. How much does the symptomatology of the boy camouflage the needs of the others? What are these needs? Why must it be Marco who is forced to protect his parents' sterile and monotonous relationship? Why is it impossible to face this?

There are as many hypotheses as there are ways at arriving at their proof. But now the time has come to find the most direct path for entering into the family, using the information at hand. The following are the initial remarks of the first therapy session:

Mother (*as the therapist enters*): Good afternoon.
Therapist (*shaking her hand*): A pleasure to meet you. . . . Was it you with whom I spoke by phone?
Mother: Yes, yes, certainly.
Therapist (*indicating Marco who is standing with one arm raised in a theatrical gesture*): Ah, you are Sitting Bull. I don't know an Indian greeting. Maybe it's, let's see, "Whoo ee" (*he gives an Indian yell*).
Marco: Who are you trying to make fun of?
Therapist: Ah . . . well, don't they do that? . . .
Marco (*in a gutteral tone*): Come on now, stop kidding around.
Therapist (*quietly chiding*): Nooo, but this is the voice of a cowboy, not the voice of an Indian! (*Father and mother are laughing.*)
Marco: Well you're wrong! This voice is the very voice of an Indian.
Therapist: From my experience you're not too good at it. Look, I've seen films about Indians for at least 12 years and I assure you that that was the voice of an old cowhand, and not very well done at that.
Marco: Well I . . .

Therapist (*interrupting him*): What's your name — not your stage name — the other one?

Marco: I don't have a stage name. I have two names.

Therapist: Tell me the first.

Marco (*emphatically*): It's the name of the sainted evangelist: Saint Mark.

Therapist: What is your most important characteristic . . . Saint Mark?

Marco: No characteristic!

Therapist: Listen, mine is the name of a martyred virgin saint; what are you?

Mother (*turning to Marco*): How well you're speaking today.

Therapist: No Ma'm. I don't find him doing well at all; he's being ridiculous. (*He turns to Marco.*) You know, a lot of interesting people come to us, but you're not even slightly interesting. In fact, I'd say you're rather boring. I was led to believe that you were creative on the subject of the Apaches; your mother clued me in. But as soon as we talk about classical themes, about the saints for instance — there's just deadly boredom.

"Deadly boredom" — the forbidden theme, never admitted by this family — was introduced by the therapist through the identified patient. It was Marco, from the beginning of the session, who functioned as the basic instrument with which both the family and the therapist sought to reach the same goal: control of the therapeutic system. In attempting to achieve this, the family system had already furnished valuable information to the therapist via the original telephone call. He was able to utilize this when anticipating his initial encounter with both patient and family.

The therapist had immediately understood the provocative quality of Marco's symptomatology and had made it the essential element for his counterprovocation. In this way he had deprived the boy of the habitual control he exerted over the family relationships by virtue of his behavior. The voluntary aspect of this was so hypertrophic that it became uncomfortable for him as well as for the others.

What might have happened had the therapist not elected to meet the challenge using the identified patient and had, instead, chosen to avoid or minimize the scrutiny of the patient's symptomatology? Surely the road would have been much longer with greatly reduced possibilities for success.

We do not wish to imply that this is the only way to enter a complex family reality, but we submit that it does simplify many things, freeing us immediately from being bound to the climate of the family, intertwined as it is with the patient's symptomatology. Other types of interventions, which avoid the impact with the symptomatology and postpone confronting the problem, would probably be slowed down by one or another family member or the patient himself who, at any "hot" moment in the session, could ask for a diagnosis, a prognosis, or a "therapy" for poor Marco.

The permanent function of the identified patient, the ultimate expression of a rigid family organization, is, for us, the *point of departure* for our work. If we begin to make our therapeutic way by attacking the function of the identified patient, we act upon the same mechanism which led him to become the scapegoat.

FROM THE FUNCTION OF THE IDENTIFIED PATIENT TO THE NETWORK OF FUNCTIONS OF THE FAMILY

The provocative intervention must bring us into communication with all of the family members by way of the same route they use for communicating among themselves: the patient. To do this it is essential that the patient be given a different function, one which radically redefines the characteristics of the "poor sick boy" so dear to the whole family. Together with defining the voluntary aspect of his behavior, the therapist must give him a *new function* as the official controller of the family, without whose dedication the others could not be able to manage.

But from where does the idea of assigning the function of family regulator to the identified patient derive? The idea comes from the family members themselves. They invariably describe how one family member controls the behavior of the others through his illness. The ambiguity of the family's message lies in the justification of this pattern as the inevitable result of the illness of the patient. This is why our principal objective is to redefine his behavior as voluntary. Clarifying his function within the family system then becomes much easier, since the family is already aware of it.

In synthesis, the therapist construes their message as having two distinct parts: 1) "He controls our behavior"; 2) "but he doesn't do it on purpose." The therapist accepts only the first part and accentuates its importance. If the function of "control" is defined as necessary and the identified patient as irreplaceable ("no one else in the family could do it as well"), the system will no longer have an excuse for continuing a relational "game" which requires a scapegoat to maintain it. Basically, the therapist states, "The identified patient is essential to the family because he *voluntarily* and *logically* behaves in ways that are *useful* to the functioning of the family." Of course, this statement cannot be administered like magic words at the end of the session, but it does represent the goal of the work of the therapist, even during the first encounter. On one hand, such an intervention provocatively reproposes that the patient is the official sentinel of the system; on the other hand, it implicitly subverts the characteristics of this role.

Using totally arbitrary points, the therapist assigns only to the identified patient the job of protecting his family from unwished for variations of behavior. By exaggerating and reinforcing the patient's function, the therapist gets the information about the family's organization which he needs to examine at a deeper level. By observing the manner in which the system transmits its uncertainties and problems, both spontaneously and during the provocation of the identified patient, the therapist becomes privy to the script of the family interaction and can then form a partial hypothesis about their functioning.

Before and during the session each person sends and responds to the messages of the therapist according to the preordained patterns of the family organization. While the identified patient "judiciously" acts out his function and the therapist begins to provoke him about this, the family visibly acts out its most peculiar behaviors.

In fact, if it is true that the provocation of the identified patient is merely a means to throw the family system out of balance and to gain intimate information on its functioning, it is also true that to do this the therapist must have glimpsed some element relative to the functions of other members of the system and to have formed, already, some *hypotheses on the relational scenario* which unites them. At this point he could connect the function of the identified patient with the functions of the others and for this reason place him in his role as the supporter of certain interactive patterns. In this way the identified patient will not be provoked as an isolated individual but rather as an integrated part of a larger system.

The therapist then arbitrarily indicates that the identified patient is the cause of many occurrences, even though he knows that the "cause" can only be attributed to the functioning of the system as a whole. However, it is easy to blame the identified patient because of his inexplicable behavior and even the therapist's initial hypotheses concerning family functioning can easily be ascribed to the will of the identified patient. In this way the therapist can formulate and test his initial hypotheses without blaming the family and without taking attention away from the identified patient.

Let us continue the case of Marco.

Therapist (*turned toward Marco*): How come you'd rather play Sitting Bull than do the things other 16-year-olds do? Or do you sometimes forget the Indians and take a rest?

Father: Always! It's always these Apaches!

Therapist (*nodding to Marco that he expects him to answer for himself*)

Father: Every time . . .

Marco (*interrupting him*): Oh, it depends . . .

Therapist: Excuse me, but I want him to answer (*indicating Marco*).

Marco: It depends on them . . . on how they bother me.

Therapist: Let's see; if they annoy you too much, you respond . . . like an Indian?

Marco: Well . . . not exactly.

Therapist: So if you act like Sitting Bull, it's because, as you see it, they do something to you that we still don't know.

Marco: They say . . . they say a lot of things to each other.

Mother (*interrupting her son and turning affably to her husband*): He's always been a bit strange, Marco, don't you think? A bit like your mother . . .

Therapist (*turned toward Marco*): But you, do you play the Indian more when you think your mother has had it with your father or when she acts resigned to everything?

Father: My wife thinks I have to be stronger with Marco.

Therapist: Look how he's getting excited, like Sitting Bull. At the very least he's thinking that his wife thinks he's a failure, never mind "stronger."

Father (*to wife*): You never thought I was very strong.

Marco (*shouting*): Is this serious, my dear man! They don't know . . . they're superficial, they're atheists. The Italian government . . . the communists . . .

Therapist (*turned toward Marco*): Oh, it's true, you have a lot to do! But whatever gave you the idea that your father wasn't satisfied to pose as a depressed failure and your mother as a smiling martyr? When did you begin to believe that if you didn't do your wretched caricatures they would kill each other?

Mother: The truth is, Marco was always apprehensive. When he was small he was obsessed by the fear that I would leave him . . .

Therapist (*to Marco*): Ah, it was then that you began to think that you were essential to the family. Maybe you weren't so wrong. . . . If you were so convinced of it, you must have had good reason. . . . Don't you think it would be a good idea to change your mind and take a rest, even for a minute?

We already mentioned how the family assumes a rapport with the therapist based on their expectation of his therapeutic function. Because of their expectations, it suits the therapist to present himself in a totally surprising function. Thus, while the parents are expecting a ponderous investigation of the reasons for the pathological behavior of their son, the therapist, instead, gives an Indian yell, invading the patient's territory from the first moments of their session. Not only does he not dispute Marco's behavior, but he also anticipates and provokes it. The redefinition of the therapeutic relationship derives from this, and it quickly tends to destabilize the organized order of the family.

Already in this opening phase, based upon the relationship the family members attempt to establish with the therapist and on their first reactions to his destabilizing interventions, the therapist obtains specific information about the family's programming and on the function assigned to each member.

The examples explored so far demonstrate how the provocation of the identified patient can work using a direct confrontation, "eye to eye" with him. In the next example we will demonstrate how the same maneuver may be effective using the obvious exclusion of that confrontation. It is important in both instances to note that the centrality of the identified patient is accentuated and not disputed. The choice of strategy is dictated, as usual, by the family, whose "style" we try to respect and emphasize. Where the identified patient tends to control the family circuit openly and actively, involving himself in all exchanges, we opt for the first technique. If control and centrality are exerted instead through self-withdrawal and refusal (of sexuality, of food, of speech), our choice becomes the second.

The father, mother, and brother of Donatella come from the south of Italy, while her husband was from Sardinia. She has been "brought north" from Calabria where she has been coddled and nurtured by her parents for the past two months. Donatella is anorectic: She is 5 feet 7 inches tall and weighs about 67 pounds. She enters the first session sustained by her mother and her brother Nunzio and says nothing. Her father and husband come in separately.

The therapist, who has observed the scene through the oneway mirror, enters carrying a large chair.

Therapist: Hello. (*turning to Donatella*) Would you mind sitting here? You seem very tired. It's hard to stand on your feet and then even more exhausting to speak. (*He seats her behind his back, excluding her totally from the circle he has created with the rest of the family.*)
Father: She is not well.
Therapist (*gesturing toward the patient behind him without turning around*): What is her name?
Mother: Donatella.

Here the attack on the role of the identified patient is made through her exclusion. Donatella's centrality, which is maintained through her showy refusal at self-nourishment and at speaking, is revealed as theatrical and is prescribed. From this point on Donatella will be provoked continually through a pattern of exclusion-inclusion. If on one hand she has been physically set apart, on the other she will always be included in the discussion without being granted the opportunity to intervene.

Therapist (*looking around*): Who is the person most worried about Donatella?
Mother (*after a moment of silence*): Her mother! (*She extends a sheet of paper toward the therapist.*) These are the tests she had done.
Therapist (*taking the list*): Am I to understand, then, that you are the one who is most anxious about your daughter?
Father: The truth is we're all worried.
Therapist: But you, sir, seem the most resigned. I get the impression that you don't believe anything much can change. From your expression I get the feeling that Donatella has succeeded in worrying her mother greatly but that you feel absolutely impotent.
Father: Well, in fact . . .
Therapist (*interrupting him and turning to the husband*): You are her husband?
Mother (*interrupting*): Yes.
Therapist: How long have you been married?
Mother (*again interrupting*): Two years and some.
Husband: Two years in May.
Therapist: Did Donatella make you feel that you were married to half a person right away?
Husband: The truth is I'm the one who feels like half a man. Donatella and I were hardly together at all in Sardinia. She spent most of her time with them instead of with me, her husband. Last year she was in a bad way and spent the whole summer in Calabria. . . . I was left alone.
Therapist: I sincerely believe that Donatella is convinced that this part of the family (*indicating her parents and brother*) could never be separated from her.
Mother: Well then she didn't have to marry. . . . It wasn't our idea . . . their marriage. (*nodding toward her husband*) They're the ones who wanted . . . against our approval. I accepted it only because my son talked me into it.

The questions, designed to differentiate the members of the family, are posed so as to imply that Donatella was acting voluntarily. From the continuous interjecting by her mother and from the preceding information, the therapist hypothesizes that Donatella's function serves to unite the two families, the old and the new. "Half a person" may signify that she is very thin or that one-half of her is with one party and one-half with the other.

The provoking of Donatella is the means for reaching others in the family—in this case the husband. He is the one who ties into the therapist's line of questioning with what concerns him most personally. At this point the therapist may say he has entered into the family system. They are, in fact, discussing real problems, not in terms of their being related only to Donatella's illness, although she may be seen as being responsible for them. Even the mother has given up talking of tests and symptoms and is admitting to difficulties within the family.

Therapist: What did your son do?

Mother: He was very persuasive.

Therapist (*turning to Nunzio*): How come you made such a mistake? What made you think your sister would really want to be separated from the rest of the family?

Brother: Well she told me she would realize herself in that way, by marrying . . .

Therapist: She fooled you.

Brother: It seemed right to try to convince my mother. After all, marrying was a choice that concerned my sister's life.

Therapist: But didn't you realize that your sister was used to playing with other people's lives?

Brother: No, it never occurred to me. (*A silence of some minutes follows.*)

Father: It's probable that we are joking with our life (*begins to weep*).

Mother: I wish I was dead! Not my son . . . not my daughter . . . I want to die. I'm already 58! It's better to die! Not to see! Not to hear!

Therapist (*turned toward the brother*): Look at that! You managed to hear your mother, who is 58, sound as if she were 88. . . . Your mother is talking as if she had one foot in the grave.

The therapist had noted that the brother acted as an intermediary in opposing situations and that his function as the "bridge" was activated whenever tension arose. Then he introduced the idea that brother may, in fact, have been the victim of the very circuit which he thought he controlled. His function as the "bridge," therefore, was seen as a means which Donatella could use at will to achieve her goals. The roles were reversed: It was not the family who had done things to put Donatella's life at risk. It was she, with her symptoms, who jeopardized the lives of the others.

Therapist (*turning again to the brother*): I really feel that the person most taken in by Donatella was you (*pointing to Nunzio*), because she convinced you that you could easily take her place at home. Your sister never for a moment thought you could take her place, but she made you think that!

Brother (*in a serious tone*): I guess I was often used by my sister.

Therapist: Not often, always!

Brother (*turning to his sister*): Am I wrong?

Therapist (*blocking his view of Donatella*): No, don't ask her because she'll never give you an adult response. The problem is that she outwitted you all around. First she led you to believe you could replace her at home, getting her share of attention from your parents, and then she went ahead and got even more attention than before with this story of not eating. I'll bet that at this point your parents can't think of you at all because all their thoughts are directed to the person dying of starvation.

Mother: That is so true! Why does she always say to me: "You love Nunzio more than me." What the doctor is saying is really true! Now I do think of my son, but I'm much more involved with her, in that condition.

With this intervention the therapist begins to investigate the relationship between brother and sister and between them and their parents. Brother is seen as never designing his own actions but active only in relationship to the exigencies of the others. There is no escape for him! If this is indeed his situation, he cannot continue to delude himself about one day breaking free of it. It is this delusion, in fact, which keeps him from changing.

Donatella is again warned not to speak but there is an implicit message: "If you wish to speak you've got to find a different way of expressing yourself." Donatella's function begins to emerge in all of its complexity. Her connections with the functions of other family members begin to be delineated.

This example demonstrates how one may induce a therapeutic crisis and force the system beyond its sphere of stability. The therapist must attribute to the symptomatic behavior a function designed to bind together the members of the system and activate that tension which heretofore was invested in the identified patient. The stress, which was all focused on her alone, has finally been redistributed among them all. The tight closure which the family had maintained to protect their interactions was used by the therapist in a manner diametrically opposed to theirs. The identified patient, who always served as the means to close themselves in, became the principal means for opening the system.

CHALLENGE TO THE FUNCTION AND SUPPORT OF THE PERSON

From the first session we try to involve the family in the therapeutic process. Each member must feel motivated to return, to commit himself to something which concerns him deeply and personally.

The principal difficulty lies in the goal of reaching each member individually and helping to get him to choose between that which he usually does and that which he would like to do, between that which is and that which he would like to have come about. Agreeing with other psychotherapists, particularly Farrelly and Brandsma (1974), we think that the idea of taking responsibility for one's own choices is very useful in psychotherapy, where there is often a tendency to consider persons as victims of incontrollable forces.

Let us continue the session with Donatella.

Donatella: I'm sick and tired of being always in the middle of everything (*begins to cry*) . . . I want my own life . . . let me be! Why do you always look toward me? I feel a tremendous weight! (*she breaks into sobs.*)

Therapist (*moving close to Donatella and sitting beside her with a hand on her shoulder*): You know, Donatella, I feel that weight but I also feel your fear . . . (*a deep silence falls*) . . . that fear that has always made you feel you need to be this broomstick (*indicating her body*) . . .
Donatella (*almost smiling*): Do you think it gives me pleasure . . .
Therapist: I know, I know. But even if you risk your life this way, you think this is the way you must pay. Even more . . . if your risking your life obliges everyone to not question anything, ever. You've all become immobile as statues . . . but this is the only way you know to keep your fears at bay.
(*Donatella nods.*)

After a few minutes of silence the therapist ends the session, setting the time of the next appointment.

In this last segment the importance of the identified patient as modulator of the intensity of the therapeutic counterprovocation is clear. The therapist may calibrate his rapport with the patient on the basis of the confirmation given to his interventions by the patient. In an early phase the therapist refuses any possibility of a dialogue, while he later accepts the exchange when the patient introduces elements which are less manipulative and more related to her suffering.

Some practical requisites which the therapist must have at his disposal in order to successfully involve the family in therapy are brilliantly expressed by Farrelly and Brandsma:

> . . . the therapist exaggerates everything beyond his everyday style. The intensity of his voice is louder than in normal conversation and everything seems amplified. There must be a strong dramatic and hyperbolic aspect in the therapy . . . the therapist will not only elaborate upon the client's responses; he will also use his own subjective reactions, his intuition and fantasy, his internal and idiosyncratic associations as material for constructing his own responses (1974).

Sometimes using vulgar language to convey his intuitions, he verbalizes the doubts and the taboos which the family members may not even permit themselves to think about. In this way he reduces the heavy weight which presses upon everything, preventing everyone from being clear and explicit.

The following is a phrase used, in session, to a famous surgeon who covered his sense of inferiority with the façade of his professional prestige: "How come that without a scalpel in your hand you always must feel that you're shit?" We maintain, in fact, that to feel anger in the face of one's weaknesses is often a stimulus toward no longer feeling oneself a victim and toward the beginning of making choices. Provoking an immediate emotional reaction, even if it is unpleasant, permits patients to respond to the therapist and to themselves in a way which is more consonant with their true emotions, avoiding the discrepancy between what one feels and what one says, which is the greatest obstacle to change.

The therapist may activate his grasp of the burdensome problems of the family through the use of provocation, the very word, in its etymology, giving us its essence — "pro-vocare," to call forth. In his challenge to the function of the patient and, through time, to the other members of the family system, he leads them to a clear definition of their needs and their individual potential. If this begins to take place, the deeply feared crisis becomes inevitable. This is difficult to arrive at with rigid family systems because of their exceptionally tight control of individual emotions, which are habitually sacrificed in the name of some undifferentiated family emotivity. In these cases, above all, nothing moves unless one creates such stress that some family member feels pressed to break with the "family loyalty" (Boszormenyi-Nagy & Spark, 1973). Someone must be made to feel that it is easier to *react in a personal and differentiated way to the therapist's provocation* than to remain the faithful actor of the old repetitive performance. The former alternative is chosen not because the therapist has smoothed the way to it, but rather because he has made the latter much more difficult to stay with.

Taking the negative half of the ambivalence which people have toward their function upon himself, the therapist carries it to the extreme consequences, forcing each one, once and for all, to plunge into the limitations and suffering which accompany these functions. Only in this way is it possible to make a choice to move toward change. This decision, like its counterpart of non-change, is of an emotional nature;

it is a sort of instinctive reaction, necessary in that moment. The clarification and understanding of why one behavior is selected over another will be examined later on.

Provocation is an extraordinarily powerful instrument for creating these emotional conditions because it allows the tension within the family to increase. The therapist then has the job of channeling this tension toward growth. Before, each family member, out of a deep fear of separation, felt compelled to represent only that function which adapted to the functions of the other family members. Now the therapist *creates an even stronger emotional intensity designed to connect their suffering and their sense of burden to the exercising of their assigned functions.* The actors in this unchanging performance are provoked on the level of their most stereotypical caricatures. Each one then finds it impossible to sustain the delusion that he is evolving within his old, assigned function. Therefore, each one must redefine himself in terms of his own ambiguity and begin making choices. Above all, the identified patient must choose between two routes: that which is coherent to the bitter end with his role as the patient, in which he can differentiate himself from the others only by way of his illness, or that in which his differentiation may come about through the expression of actions independent of the function assigned to him.

The following is an example of how the function of the identified patient as connected with the functions of the others becomes the ideal emotional instrument for forcing the patient to define himself.

Alberto, a 20-year-old heroin addict, is seated silently between his parents. His expression is one of guilt and shame. His father, mother, and older sister are unable to focus attention on anything but him, caught in the power of his mood. All seem paralyzed by his presence.

Therapist(*taking a plastic syringe from his pocket and showing it to Alberto*): Whom do you help the most with this?
Alberto (*after a long silence*): I don't understand.
Therapist (*placing the syringe in Alberto's hand*): Whom do you help the most with this? (*A tense silence of several minutes' duration falls over everyone.*)
Alberto: My father.

Father: That's how you help me?!

Therapist (*taking the syringe from Alberto and giving it to father*): How?

Father (*annoyed*): How what?

Therapist: Your son—he thought of helping you. How do you think he wants to help you?

Father: I really don't think I need help!

Therapist (*giving the syringe to the mother*): Your husband seems to be angry with me . . . he doesn't intend to help me understand.

Father: But I . . . you're wrong!

Therapist (*interrupting*): Your turn is over . . . let's hear what your wife has to say.

Mother: Maybe . . . Alberto thinks that my husband . . . you know, at home I've always done everything . . . he never understood me, not even when I needed him . . . (*begins to weep*).

Therapist (*handing the syringe to sister*): Let's hear what you have to say.

Sister (*shaking the syringe up high*): First of all, he helps papa to understand that when he uses this . . . he is like papa when he drinks!

It is clear that the family now has sufficient motive to return to the next session. The therapy room has become a place where deep tensions and differences have surfaced. These cannot be covered up with the usual ease, nor can they possibly have resolved anyone's problem. It becomes difficult, then, to abandon this room.

The family becomes enmeshed by the force of the provocation, which personally challenges each member. The challenge is such that its attraction is unavoidable. That attraction derives from the fact that the patient and the family can no longer maintain the confusion that habitually reigns among them, nor can they maintain their rigid functions. Every time the therapist attacks their functions and forces them to identify themselves with their functions, each one is helpless in continuing to confound the behavior manifested with the individual who is manifesting it. At that point it is they themselves who reveal a dignity and an autonomy which they had previously buried.

ARE WE OR ARE WE NOT SYSTEMIC?

Given the fact that our kind of provocative intervention has sometimes been criticized as "asystemic," we think it valuable to explore certain aspects of our intervention that may explain our method of provoking families.

The therapist substitutes for the identified patient, taking the central role. From the episodes already reported, we see clearly how the therapist literally steals the "driver's seat" in the family until the family no longer has the need for a "director" for its survival. Until that time, however, the therapist remains the functional mediator of family tensions, as was the identified patient before him; however, while the patient served the role of maintaining the family organization, the therapist serves to break it up. While the patient's behavior, even in its diversity, was predictable, the therapist is totally spontaneous and unpredictable. Even when he is urged to participate on the level of the rational and comprehensible and to give a diagnosis of the family's problems, he uses a totally unpredictable intervention, so as not to touch the ambiguous territory of irrationality assigned to the behavior of the patient. It is this same unpredictability which prohibits the restructuring of static interrelational functions. His centrality then becomes one of the more disturbing elements to the stasis of the system.

During the initial and intermediate phases of therapy, provocation is used often. The therapist seeks to render the situation even weightier, pointing up the incommunicability of the family, so instead of encouraging verbal interaction he impedes it. While on one hand he makes felt the necessity for a direct confrontation among the family members, on the other hand he guarantees the impossibility of this by remaining the only interlocutor for each one. This might raise the suspicion that this approach is lacking in respect for the systemic view that interaction is the principal key to intervention. However, in every dyadic exchange between the therapist and a family member, provocative elements for other components of the family are also introduced. The therapist says, for example, while turned toward a brother of the patient, "Anna has fixed in her mind that she has a deathly fear of taking personal responsibility out of the house, away from her parents' protection and affection." Using a strongly provocative tack, the therapist challenges Anna's brother on the problem of breaking away but at the same time:

1) He maintains his provocation of Anna to whom he attributes thoughts and actions without having questioned her.
2) He gives a different definition of her relationship with her brother.
3) He includes the parents in this mechanism, who, even in the hope of doing good, sustain this situation.

There is something to challenge all of them. In an apparently dyadic exchange between the therapist and brother, from which all of the others seem to be excluded, each one is provoked along a line of thought which draws him or her into gripping relationship with the others. It is, however, a silent interaction which develops in intensity the more that it has been simultaneously solicited and impeded. If initially it was the family which avoided any action dealing with their deep problems in an attempt to keep tensions within bearable limits, it is now the therapist who will claim the right to disrupt their pattern.

Let us refer to Marco's case, where the therapist asks, "But you, do you play Indian more when you think your mother has had it with your father or when she acts resigned to everything?", or further on, " . . . whatever gave you the idea that your father wasn't satisfied to pose as a depressed failure? . . . When did you begin to believe that if you didn't do your wretched caricatures they would kill each other?" Or when working with the family with an alcoholic father, the therapist asks the son, "When did you begin to develop the worry that your mother would fall into despair if your father drank?" These are all examples of *triadic activation*, where each phrase binds three people together with arbitrary definitions of each one's function.

It is understood that the choice of the definition derives from the specific personality of the therapist, but it is just that which makes it possible to be *associated with the family, participating in the therapeutic process.* That is to say, the therapist's participation draws upon the elements gathered from each family member, the emotions which each one elicits and the intensity with which he feels connected to all of this. If he then succeeds in bringing together the family's "story" in a different but equally credible and intense emotional framework, both therapist and family will participate together in the construction of a new system.

We have heard it said many times that one intervention is systemic and another is not or even that this is "more systemic" than that, in a logic in which the judging of "systemic" seems based more on the degree of asceticism the therapist demonstrates toward the family than on the respect for a circular model. The premise for certain of those affirmations seems to consist in the fact that the more distant the therapist remains from the emotions raised during sessions, the less he runs the risk of falling into a linear logic. That position raises the suspicion that it is not taken with the goal of being coherent with a systemic model but from the fear of not being so. It is possible that those comments derive from a schism between "systemic thought" and "linear feeling," the two being hardly compatible.

Only if we consider the individual as an emerging process who always has the possibility of manifesting diversity, can we freely utilize our emotions in rapport with the behavior of this one or that one, according to a criterion in which that quality to be provoked is the *manifestation and not the object* (Dell, 1980). But if by misfortune, even professing ourselves systemic therapists, we confound the manifestation with the object, the idea that the manifestations of an individual are inherent only to him may take root. That is why we try to change him in place of the function he serves or that which he says or does, remaining blocked in a digital frame of reference where the object has changed or hasn't changed. If, instead, we really feel the enormous difference between saying *he is crazy* and saying *his behavior is crazy,* we can calmly attack his symptomatic function and those things tied to it without fear of being judged insufficiently systemic—and we don't risk remaining sadly trapped in a cause-effect circuit.

Our kind of therapy is analogous to the mode of many families, simply because families act in ways which are neither linear nor circular.

If gesture, language, silence, humor, dramatics, etc. can serve as instruments, arms of manipulation for the family, for what reason must we appear unarmed? If Marco causes us grief by playing Indian, why should we be ashamed to respond in the same key? If the patient can move around the room threatening his father with his finger pointed at him, we may do the same with the patient, as long as it is part of a therapeutic plan. Clearly, this involves a high degree of personal exposure and, at bottom, of risk, but if the therapist does not risk anything, how can the family?

Another point is made by those who, *worried about the level of tension* created during the session, ask if this does not have a destructive effect on the family and, in particular, on the patient. We respond that our work effects a redirecting of the tension which the family already carries, redistributing it among its members so that, if on one level tension increases, on another it can be contained more easily just because the therapist alters the quality of the tension. Moreover, we can no longer view the patient as the personification of fragility, nor do we believe that certain functions served by him and his family members have any hope of evolving in a protective situation. The problem, if it exists, rests in the aforementioned sense of not confusing the functions with the individuals who serve them. It is our duty, therefore, *to attack the former while sustaining the latter, scrupulously avoiding doing the contrary* (Menghi, 1977).

Two people, a patient and his illness, are lying in a bed. His doctor enters the room blindfolded. He is holding a cudgel. Once beside the bed he begins to strike blindly at the man and at his illness. I don't recall exactly who died first, victim of these blows . . . but it seems to me it was the patient (de Alarcon, 1978).

CHAPTER 5

Strategic Denial as
Homeostatic Reinforcement

TO UNITE OR SEPARATE?

The provocation intervention is explicitly active and commits the therapist to direct confrontation with the family. Our experience has taught us that it is useful to alternate this approach with another which seems in opposition, that is, to anticipate and neutralize the possible relapse of the family.

The two-leveled message which we have hypothesized as a therapeutic response to the paradoxical demands of the family — "yes, I help you by not helping you" — may be put into practice in a specific intervention which we call *strategic denial*. This is a paradoxical technique in which the therapist clearly allies himself with the homeostatic element in the system, unearthing and amplifying the bases for the impossibility of change. The therapist, for example, may say, seeing a patient who appears visibly improved, "What's happening now is very

71

dangerous. Your child is telling you that he doesn't have to throw tantrums anymore. But this might be even more serious because he knows he can't control himself for too long. It's understandable that you (indicating the patient) want to confuse your family. What upsets me is that you're also trying to confuse me."

The family finds itself with a therapist who has taken over their deepest fears and come around to the belief that nothing can really change, denying the possibility of improvement.

By denying visible improvements, the therapist has accomplished a number of operations. He has reconfirmed the functional significance of the symptom. He has provoked the identified patient, underscoring his role as the homeostatic pole of the therapeutic system. But, above all, he has anticipated the relapse of the family in its attempt to reorder itself in the old pattern.

In this sense, denial is akin to the situation of the disciple in Koan Zen who, as a novitiate, is given an impossible task by his master: "If you hold your head low, I will strike you; if you raise it, I will strike you." It is as if the denial of any solution transforms the disciple. Similarly, strategic denial moves the family to challenge the therapist's homeostatic stance. By trying to show him a less pessimistic view of their evolution, the family may work out a way to rearrange and restructure the rules and definitions which maintain their status quo.

The formation of the therapeutic relationship, the improvement of the identified patient, a change in the functional intertwining within the family, the end of therapy, or a request for therapy again after an interruption—all are points in the process where denial may be a catalyst for reconsidering what has been happening. It may be a point of departure for the family's new self-searching.

For this intervention to be successful an intense relationship between the family and the therapist must exist. That relationship must then become the essential framework for strategic denial (Napier & Whitaker, 1978). If it is not anchored in the therapeutic union, it may seem a mechanical maneuver capable of damaging the family, since they may perceive it as the therapist's indifference toward their problems or his inability to understand them.

For a therapist who chooses to look at the family from within, *entering and distancing himself from the family space* are inseparable and inevitable moments he must face. Denial of the therapy or the barely achieved object permits the therapist to stand back from what he has activated, thus giving the family a problem to solve which is not directly mediated by his presence.

Just as he had actively built up the relationship with the patient, so does he now appear to withdraw from what occurs. In reality he has merely changed his mode of participating. In fact, the family gets the message that he understands their difficulty but he has removed himself as the agent of change, challenging them to take hold of the management of their own problems. He relinquishes his role as a protagonist to become an observer of the initiatives which the family undertakes.

The process of alternating the times of participation, where he enters the emotional space of the family (provocation), with periods of separation, when he leaves that space (denial), resembles the movement of a pendulum. The arcs of oscillation, in opposition to each other, are also complementary: The movement in one direction has its own significance, but it is indispensable to the contrary movement. These cycles have a bearing on the tension which exists within the therapeutic system.

During the phase of provocation the therapist is directly involved vis-à-vis the identified patient and the family, but through denial he leaves his central position and moves to a more peripheral space from which to observe family movements. In the former phase, the tension affects the *heart of the therapist-family rapport.* In the latter phase, it becomes completely redistributed *within the family group,* developing all their potential for transformation and differentiation (Nicolo & Saccu, 1979). Only because the therapist is able to change the quality of the tension through his intervention of provocation can the family now more readily contain and digest it.

An illustration will more easily trace the cycles of the pattern of participation-separation (see Figure 4). In this we see that point B represents the maximum engagement (participation) of the therapist within the therapeutic system. It is also the point where maximum tension exists and where the therapist begins to brusquely distance (separate) himself from the family. The sequencing of his participation-separation over time reflects the evolution of the progress made from preceding cycle (A, B, A_1, B_1), etc. The passage from one cycle to the next em-

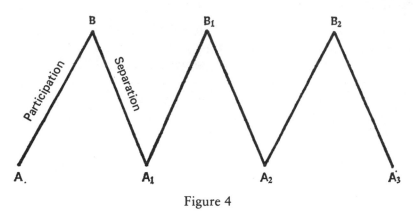

Figure 4

bodies a progressive increase in complexity and differentiation within the therapeutic system until the point of final separation, when the therapeutic system itself separates into its individual components.

The family, however, may at first deny the efficacy of the therapy sessions or the fact that an objective was achieved (for example, a true improvement in the symptomatology). They may completely delegate the responsibility for change to the therapist. Doing this, they appear once again as a passive object in the hands of someone who is working wholeheartedly for change, only to be faced by a group dedicatedly united toward demonstrating their total impotence. Thus, a sort of tug-of-war is created between the family and the therapist, wherein both forces are immobilized by their equal but opposing positions.

If the therapist suddenly lets go of the rope, the family finds itself off balance and must take a position of active involvement which earlier had been delegated to the therapist. Strategic denial, in effect, may be compared to "letting go of the rope" by the therapist, who acts anticipating the moves the family is preparing to make.

THE DENIAL OF THE NEED FOR THERAPY

The initial phases of a therapeutic process generally represent a period of mutual adaptation on the part of the family and the therapist. As we have seen in preceding chapters, this adaptation is predetermined by the expectations each one has of the other. The decision to seek therapy may have required such tight cohesion that the family sacrifices the personal motivation of each member. If this is so, the physical presence of individual members may be merely that. They may be removed from the idea of getting deeply involved and refuse to consider themselves possible activators of change. Many families communicate this message in their first telephone contact.

The mother of an 18-year-old drug addict called us to set up an appointment. She quickly told us that hers was a happy and united family but that her husband, an important businessman, would not be able to attend the sessions even though the idea for therapy was his. She added that she couldn't understand why her 12-year-old daughter should have to be exposed to the "repercussions" of the family therapy, but, in any case, she was disposed to set up a first appointment. We said no, marveling at her request. We understood that, willing it herself, she would have been able to convince all the family to participate. We said that such a happy family, with only one problem, didn't really justify our intervention, which would certainly be disturbing. Taken aback by our response, she said that if it was really necessary she would take it upon herself to bring the entire family. We refused again, adding that we would be convinced of their willingness to participate only if each individual member of the family called us. Each one did call. We then played the devil's advocate, advising each one not to enter the therapeutic situation unless he or she had his/her own solid motivation for doing so. It was only after they expressed their personal reasons for seeking therapy that we made an appointment. Our repeated denial, starting with the first contact, had the effect of each one's making a strong connection with us, reversing a situation which seemed lost before it even started.

The more rigid the family organization is, the more useful denial is when brought into play early in the process. We have found that temporizing about arriving at a clearer definition can be self-defeating. The danger is that the family members may turn away just at the moment that they realize they must each accept personal responsibility. It may seem precipitous and even hostile to deny help from the earliest contact but, in fact, it can shorten the time of therapy by immediately making it clear that we cannot accept demands by proxy or contradictory messages.

Looking at it another way, if we accept the expectations of the family members, we reinforce their tendency to consolidate their forces in their preexisting static condition. By strategically denying therapy because it is "too fraught with danger for the equilibrium of a family presenting such unity," we catch them off guard, since they are expecting the therapist to do everything possible to achieve the impossible. We redefine their respective expectations. Here is an example:

The Giovine family—father, mother, and two sons—request therapy because the parents, both doctors, are concerned about their 21-year-old son who has dropped out of school and does nothing but lie about, depressed and hypochondriacal. They have searched everywhere for the right "magician" who would work wonders, but every attempt at therapy has been flatly refused. They all agreed that the only disturbing note in their idyllic peace is Ferdinand's attitude. They deny the presence of any conflict in the family in euphemistic and exaggeratedly courteous terms. To seek therapy, with mother, the undisputed leader, guiding them, is the greatest effort they can make. The dialogue begins after mother has most competently described her son's depression, his somatizing of his problems, and his hypochondria.

Mother: I feel guilty. He's like an anorectic child. We say "eat, eat" and he never does. My son doesn't study. He's often depressive. Perhaps it is my fault. What do *you* think, Doctor?

Therapist: Discussing guilt doesn't interest me. What I don't understand is why you've come to Rome.

Mother: I don't know what you mean. We don't know anything. You must tell us what to do. Right now we're at our wits' end.

Therapist: From a certain point of view it's better not to know anything. I don't believe I can help you since I'm not a magician. But if you help me to understand better or to be of some use to you, you would go home much more shaken up than when you arrived. This kind of help is risky, you know.

Father: This is interesting. Ferdinand says he was dragged here. He always lets himself get dragged along.

Therapist: And who does he resemble most in this?

Father: Me. My wife is the leader here.

Mother (*annoyed*): Some people have one personality and some another.

Ferdinand: Listen, in this family you can never say what you think. Whatever I say is interpreted as an attack. It's better to shut up.

Therapist: I agree with you. The truth is that you all "shut up." I don't see how we can possibly begin therapy because you (*to Ferdinand*) have to convince everyone that you have problems, that you have illnesses. You really enjoy the role, deep down, but the other thing is no one else could do it instead of you. Who could possibly take your place if you weren't here?

Ferdinand (*acidly*): Well . . . maybe my father. We're the most alike.

Father: I generally try to do things not to annoy anyone and . . .

Therapist: I really thing it's useless to continue. We can't count only on your mother's energy and drive. . . . If we accept that Ferdinand's life is a failure you could go on this way forever with your mother so essential to it. Your father has his hobbies, his profession. Your little sister has her school etc., etc.

Mother: Listen, doctor, do you know that my husband has been sick for six years. He's very nervous. It might be Parkinson's Disease. I don't know where to turn first.

Father (*visibly upset*): Let's cut this out! The truth is my wife always thought of me as a piece of wood. She has no respect for me professionally. From the time we were at the university she was the "star." I finished med school because she pushed me. She likes to mix in everywhere and she always feels so superior. Once and for all, let's say it the way it is. I don't know if this is useful, doctor, but we four almost never talk like we're doing today.

The expectations of the family are upset by the repeated denial of the usefulness of therapy. Strategic denial also anticipates and neutralizes their repetitious pattern of interrupting and invalidating every therapeutic experience.

The therapist appears to accept their literal statement, "Quiet and harmony reign in this family," and he appears reluctant to disturb the family peace without their "essential help and authorization." This denial disorients the family, weakens its usual power structure, and forces all of the family members to probe the depths of an ambiguous situation. The therapist's refusal to enter into collusion with the family or to courteously pretend to attempt to change the situation pushes them to the crossroads: to truly work with the therapist or to leave the session.

THE DENIAL OF IMPROVEMENT

Improvement reflects a period of great instability in the course of the therapeutic process. The therapeutic team itself may feel that this is the proper phase in which to stabilize the evolution of the process. It may happen that the balance in the participation-separation rapport may tilt in favor of a more active and continuing participation by the therapist. Thus he runs the risk of taking the initiative from the family and getting caught in the seductive trap of partial and temporary improvement.

At this stage the family no longer represents a united front, but a new incongruity arrives on the scene: If the patient shows a real improvement, the rest of the family may see this as a deterioration, despite the clear evidence to the contrary. On one hand, the family reflects its progress through the improvement in the identified patient, their official spokesman; on the other hand, it is impossible for them to admit the improvement.

The therapeutic strategy of reinforcing improvement through denial of it derives from such premises. Ongoing improvement is redefined as a worsening of the situation, which supports the idea that it is better not to change anything.

The therapeutic intervention focuses on urging the family members to maintain their stability just when the first changes are visible, making them glimpse the dangers inherent in changing their rules. Once again the system is attacked through the identified patient, who is now challenged through his improvement. In reality this challenge reinforces the system's tendency toward change through the *explicit non-acceptance of the improvement* (Searles, 1961).

We have observed that explicitly recognizing improvement in the patient in this phase often is countered by the family's renewed emphasis of even the most minimal difficulty the patient has and by a denial of the results reached. After asking ourselves the possible reasons for such a response, we have hypothesized that improvement carries a sensation of threat to the family at the interactive level (Searles, 1961). If the therapist, once again, veers toward homeostasis before the family does so, the family will ultimately feel committed to getting back on their therapeutic path even if it leads to other conflicts and new problems.

Another tactic which we have found useful is to define the *improvement itself as dangerous*. In this very delicate phase there is much ambivalence toward the dual possibilities of changing (differentiation) or remaining static (cohesion). The ambivalence is no longer lodged only in the identified patient and his symptom, but is now at the level of the function of each family member. Therefore, speaking of the risks implicit in change and encouraging the release of fantasies with their related fears allow the time and space to make "the worst possible results" concrete so that they lose their destructive character (Napier & Whitaker, 1978).

Descriptions of our interventions are sometimes accompanied by the prescription: "Do not change." In this we solicit the continuation of the behaviors which accentuate the symptomatic function and the dysfunctional rules of the system. This strategy, which has already been described by many authors (Haley, 1973; Watzlawick et al., 1967; Selvini-Palazzoli et al., 1978), is presented as a necessary precaution to prevent a change which may threaten the family. Paradoxically, it works to sustain the improvement already under way and to stimulate a new cohesion within the family group. They now have to show, "up front," that they can, in fact, change.

Let us look at a case in point:

Elsa was a 15-year-old with serious anorexia. She was the only daughter of a politician. She had stopped normal eating four years earlier, took emetics continually, and almost never left the house. The only exchanges she had were with her mother, an intelligent woman, frustrated in her relationship with her husband. Two nightmares weighed upon them: the mental deterioration of the paternal grandmother, heart and soul of the paternal family (a patriarchal family from the south of Italy), and the physical deterioration of the father, afflicted with chronic leukemia. In the preceding session the therapist had provoked the patient in her function as the link between her parents and in her role of continuing the paternal branch of the family.

The symbols of death implicit in her symptomatology were, in fact, a way to express her father's most serious illness, which no one dared mention, as well as the arteriosclerosis affecting the grandmother, around whom the entire family system pivoted.

At this point in therapy the mother is in the process of establishing greater closeness with her husband's family and with her mother-in-law in particular. The nuclear and the extended families are establishing new boundaries and Elsa and her parents are doing the same. The therapy sessions have brought about noticeable improvement in the girl's symptomatology, as well as in relations between the parents themselves and among the family members in general. The therapist now decides to deny the improvement and, to emphasize the paradoxical aspects involved, he holds a lunch session. The whole family is curious and excited and actively participates in the preparation of this special meal.

Elsa says how hungry she is, as if communicating that her eating problem is a thing of the past. This observation moves the therapist to intervene quickly.

Therapist: In reality this isn't a serious meal. It's only a sort of rehearsal. (*turning to Elsa*) And what's that?
Elsa: That's my main course. I'll just put it on the side.
Therapist: You mean you eat spaghetti and then your main dish?
Elsa: I eat them separately: first the spaghetti and then the main dish.
Therapist: Right! I understand. But do you vomit before or after you eat?
Elsa: No, I don't vomit. Lately something has really changed. In fact, if I feel a bit faint I go . . .
Therapist: Mm, exactly what I was thinking, I'm not really convinced about you . . .
Elsa: I've eaten apple pie, pizza . . .
Therapist: . . . I've never seen you this way. . . . You've put on a couple of ounces, or am I mistaken?
Elsa: Yes.
Therapist: Wonderful (*ironically*).
Elsa: Thank you. (*The family laughs.*)
Therapist: You didn't understand what I meant by "wonderful."
Elsa (*in a small voice*): Why?

Therapist: Because I don't believe you'll ever do what your uncle does. When he wants spaghetti, he eats it and doesn't give a damn if he gets a paunch. But you, you've put on a couple of ounces just to confuse matters, and it's not the first time. Why do you, all of a sudden, eat more now, when you feel faint. That's what grown-ups do. . . . You can't do that, you know.

Elsa: Well, even if you say no, I hope, I believe I'm getting better.

Therapist: The miracle of San Gennaro! Excuse me, but what has changed that's letting you get better . . . that's letting you stop doing what you did for so long?

Elsa: For example, I've started to see my cousin again. When I was sick I was always alone. Now I'm starting to see kids my own age and I'm just more open . . .

Therapist: That's secondary, nothing's happened here, inside, with you (*indicating the rest of the family*).

Elsa: I don't think our family can change much . . .

Therapist: Well, then? In a way I think you're crazier now than you were before. At least before you had a reason. You were the only one who understood clearly how necessary you were to your family and how everyone used you. You have an important function. You're the interlocutor between one part of your family and the other. How could your parents speak to each other without you . . . and now you want me to think your problems have disappeared and you're getting better?

Elsa: They haven't disappeared, but something is changing.

Therapist: Nothing more needs to happen and do you know why? You know that nothing has changed at home . . . when you're all at dinner. (*to the parents*) Isn't that so?

Mother: My husband eats very fast. He eats fast because he needs to . . .

Father: I eat fast because I'm on the run to do . . .

Mother: He's interested in simple things, things he can do quickly that let him go to bed early.

Father: The truth is that sometimes I'd like to go out for some air in the evening. I go for coffee or a drink. Most of the time I go by myself because Elsa takes so long to finish eating. I ask my wife to come with me but she feels she has to stay with Elsa, at home.

Mother: You think I'm tied to her, but that attitude bothers me.

Father: If Elsa's alone in the house, at about 10:30 my wife begins to say "we have to go home." That really gets me and so I'd rather go out alone.

Therapist (*to Elsa*): Now do you understand why it's crazy to even try to get better? Do you understand why you have to remain a dopey kid and only think about how many ounces you eat and how many you vomit? Nobody here can manage without you.

A series of denials is adopted in this fragment, utilizing the material presented by the patient as new proof of her improvement. From the very beginning, the therapist refuses to accept the evidence ("I've never seen you this way . . . "), and in so doing he stimulates Elsa to defend her successes ("No, I don't vomit; lately something has really changed." "Well, even if you say not, I hope, I believe I'm getting better").

The provocation given by the therapist with his question, "How could your parents speak to each other without you?", clearly implies that a change tied to the commitment of *all* the members of the system is highly improbable. But it is just that very question which causes the parents to bring their difficulties into the open.

In a different context the therapist's question might seem an accusation, but here it expresses his emotional acceptance of whatever choice the family may make, even if this will be a return to the symptomatic choice.

TOWARD THE DISMANTLING OF THE
THERAPEUTIC SYSTEM

At a certain point the family shows its readiness to test its autonomy independent of the support of the therapist, and the therapeutic process moves toward a gradual resolution. When this happens the therapist may openly side with the family's changes and reassure the family about their accomplishments. In every stage of transition, however, fear of the unknown and very real difficulties may induce the family to return to old patterns. They may be opposed to the dissolution of the therapeutic system and may fall back into situations which justify more therapy, but which impede the process of increasing autonomy which is under way. If the therapist decides to go with the family and continue the intervention, he will be allowed to function solely as a stabilizing element.

Cohesion was initially achieved with the patient as the center. Through the course of the therapeutic process cohesion was maintained with the therapist as the new homeostatic regulator of the system. That is why the family, at this point, must accept the dissolution of the therapist-family system and attempt to stabilize its own new organization.

This is illustrated in Figure 5. In phase A the family is organized around the identified patient. In phase B it is reorganized around the therapist. If it is not able to achieve phase C, with separation from the therapist, it will try to stabilize in phase B. The end of the therapeutic process must be facilitated by the therapist through the dissolution of the preceding organization, phase B.

Faced with the family's wish to continue the sessions, often expressed by the statement, "there are still matters to be resolved; if you don't stay with us the patient may relapse," the therapist may continue in the relationship, *but* he must deny his own therapeutic function. He could respond by saying, "Yes, I'll see you all in two months, but only if you're able to help yourselves and if the patient is well." In the follow-up session the illness will no longer serve as the family's instrument for maintaining rapport with the therapist.

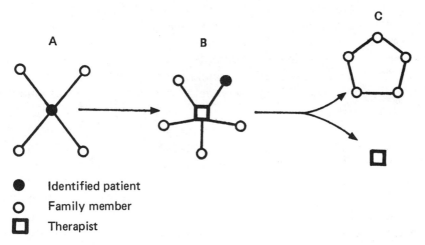

●   Identified patient
○   Family member
□   Therapist

Figure 5

Let us look at the case of a family where a satisfactory conclusion appeared to have been reached after four months of therapy.

Having summed up the situation and evaluated the results, the therapist had asked the family to come back in three months. This interval was to serve as a period in which to consolidate gains and resolve some difficulties which had surfaced during the last few sessions. The session would take place only if each one had positively applied his commitment to the goals which were mutually agreed upon. If not, the session would be postponed. In this way the family was induced to see the therapist only to tell him that, in fact, they had no further need of him. The following are some sequences from the follow-up session:

Therapist (*smiling*): The last time we met was . . .
Father: We met . . .
Mother: In November . . .
Laura: Yes, the first week of November.
Therapist: Then three months have gone by. Have you followed the rule about coming back only if each of you is satisfied with the progress that's been made?
Father: Yes. After all, we are serious people.
Therapist: Can you demonstrate your seriousness?
Father (*seeking guidance*): What task are you going to give us?
Therapist (*smiling*): I want you to conduct the session this time. I am just going to watch and observe what improvements you have made.
Father: We have made improvements . . .
Laura: Can I write them on the blackboard?
Therapist: Why not? Just the way we did before. It helps us remember them better.
Father: First of all, write down our relationships. The relations between Mom and Dad. (*to his wife*) We are getting along much better. There's more discussion between us. When a problem comes up, we talk about it, we argue about it, and we solve it. I think my wife and I are more mature than we were. Anyway, we are on the right road.
Therapist (*good-humoredly*): I bet you were the kind of student who got top grades on exams!

Father: Me? No . . . and relations with our daughters are . . .

Therapist (*to the father*): Wait a minute, please don't go so fast. We were talking about you and your wife. (*to the mother*) Mrs. De-Angeli, what do you think about this?

Mother: Oh, I agree with my husband, especially now that we have more dialogue.

Therapist: You mean that you talk . . .

Mother: Yes.

Therapist: Before you talked less . . .

Mother: Much less. We didn't talk about little things or about important things. Now, maybe we don't agree on some things, but we find a way of getting along anyway.

Therapist (*expressing incredulity*): You have managed to do this in just three months?

Mother: We had already begun earlier . . .

Therapist: That's true. You mean that you have consolidated the improvements.

Mother: Yes, exactly.

Father: Particularly in these last months, with everyone contributing.

Therapist: Do you mean including the grandmothers?

Father: No, I'm really referring to our family. We don't talk much about the grandmothers anymore.

Mother: But some relations have been broken off pretty abruptly. That bothers me somewhat.

Therapist: For example?

Mother: For example, with my mother.

Therapist: Don't you ever see her?

Mother: Rarely.

Therapist: When was the last time you saw her?

Mother: At Christmas.

Father: Yes, we were with her on Christmas Day. Now we do other things on Sundays. I take the older girls to a soccer game, or else we all go to the mountains.

Therapist (*to Laura and Marina*): Do you like watching soccer games?

Laura and Marina (*together*): Oh, yes, we love it.

Therapist: Before, you didn't go to soccer games or to the mountains! Isn't that true?

Father: I went to watch soccer by myself.

Mother: And I stayed home and faced . . .

Therapist (*to the mother*): Now that you stay home with just Claudia you have more peace and less work to do.

Mother: That's right.

Therapist: And when you go to the mountains, who goes? Just the family?

Laura: No, we go with other people.

Father: We go with friends.

Therapist: You didn't do that before.

Laura: We used to go alone, just the family used to go, and it was less fun.

Therapist: Oh! So now you go with other families, with other kids your age!

Laura: Yes.

Therapist: I think you once told me that all your friends were younger than you. Do I remember correctly?

Laura: Yes, that's right.

Therapist: But now you have friends your own age . . .

Laura: Yes, I have girlfriends and boyfriends, both.

Therapist: They're mixed.

Laura (*laughing*): Yes.

Mother: And even the invitations are . . .

Therapist: Mixed! (*Everyone laughs.*)

Mother: She gets invitations . . . I don't know . . . like to go out for pizza on Saturday night.

Therapist: I'm afraid the blackboard isn't big enough. Where will we manage to write everything? You have already talked about so many things. You certainly have been busy lately . . .

Mother: Since Christmas.

Therapist: Oh, yes. Now I remember getting a phone call that I didn't like at all, but I don't remember when it was.

Mother: Early in December.

Father: Yes, that was a bad moment.

Therapist: I'm really glad that I didn't agree to see you earlier, when things weren't going so well. I would have deprived you of the satisfaction of getting over a difficult period by your own efforts.

And we would have broken an important rule: We are supposed to see each other only to talk about improvements. (*to the father*) And your mother?

Father: My mother . . .

Therapist: Where is she living?

Father: At home . . .

Therapist: And what about boundaries?

Father: I think there's been an improvement. She keeps out of things more. The credit goes to my wife, because she has learned to accept her the way she is.

Therapist: What else is new?

Laura: Between me and Marina.

Therapist: What do you mean?

Laura (*with satisfaction*): Things are all right now. We don't fight anymore.

Therapist: How did that come about? You used to fight like cats and dogs.

Laura: You know, sometimes I used to fight on purpose. I mean I did it because I was coming here, so I thought I should do it. But now I realize that if I fight, I do it for myself and my sister, so . . .

Therapist (*to Marina*): What do you think about this?

Marina: Laura is much nicer to me now.

Therapist (*smiling*): Explain that to me. Do you mean that Laura isn't bossy anymore, or have you become bossier?

Marina: Well, a little of both.

Therapist (*to the parents*): What has happened with your plans to move to Teramo?

Father: The plan still exists, but . . .

Mother: We have to get ready for it, because I would be alone with the children all day, and if certain relationships don't improve . . .

Therapist: They still need improvement. You are worried about having all the responsibility for the children, right?

Mother: Certainly.

Laura (*catching on immediately*): Should I write down the improvements we have already made or the ones we still have to work out?

Therapist: Here's what you can do. Divide the blackboard in half. In the upper part you can write the things you have already done, and below give us a program that we can talk about at our next meeting five months from now, before the summer.

It is the family itself that indicates how to carry on. As often happens, it is Laura, the identified patient, who points the way to further progress. The blackboard records both the family's achievements and its new goals.

By setting a date several months away for the next session, the therapist lets the family feel that the therapeutic system still exists. But at this point, the family has become its own therapist, and has much less need of an external guide. If the therapist is certain that the family has achieved a new organization adequate to managing its own problems, even a relapse is not enough reason to resume the sessions. The therapist must not, in fact, lend himself to the delusion that he is so essential to a family group's evolution. He is only important at this moment because he is temporary. In these cases it seems important to us that we refuse to resume therapy, defining the relapse as an attempt by the family to place us back in a role already left behind.

The case we describe below illustrates the *denial of the relapse,* wherein the therapist tries to reinforce the results achieved, prodding the family toward the definitive dissolution of the therapeutic system.

This family was in therapy for two-and-a-half years because of the schizophrenic symptomatology presented by Maria, their middle child. At the beginning of therapy the situation seemed tragic, with the three children, Giovanna, 32 years old, Maria, 29, the identified patient, and Franco, 18 years old, totally dependent on their parents. Their emotional life and all their relationships were confused and locked within the family boundaries. In the first phase of therapy, Maria, engaged in a test of strength with the therapist, regressed painfully and spent two long months in bed, encopretic, enuretic, and forcefed. She gradually improved along with the rest of the family and some real changes occurred in their family life. The parents, now retired, enjoyed closer exchanges and every once in a while took a vacation. Each of the three children tried personally to work out their problems with work and social situations. Giovanna, the eldest, started teaching in a town away from Rome to which she then moved. Franco was actively involved with a political party and Maria had returned to her university courses while working part-time. Two years had passed since the last session with the therapist when Giovanna suddenly called to say that Maria was having a relapse. "Maria is very nervous and is insisting that she must go into a psychiatric facility." The mother, who was on vacation in her home town, was urgently called to return to Rome by the father.

More detailed and accurate questioning by telephone brought the news of a strange, sad event: Giovanna had had a relationship with a colleague for two years. They were planning marriage when a fulminating cancer caused his death a few months earlier. Giovanna reacted with great control and reserve, but right after this happened Maria became "nervous" again.

The therapist hypothesized that the so-called relapse of Maria into her old symptomatology would act as a cover for not dealing with a very real problem. It would prevent Giovanna and the family from feeling the depths of their pain and grief.

The therapist therefore decided to see the family, who confirmed his hypothesis.

All family members were present at the session but they had left a seat empty among them. The therapist construed this as a metaphoric message from the family.

Therapist: Well, do you know whose chair this is?
Father: It's yours, doctor, isn't it?
Therapist: Oh, no! I'll take this other one. This chair belongs to the person who feels worst. The person suffering the most should sit there. (*The therapist speaks in terms of suffering, not of sickness.*)

(*Maria rises and slowly occupies the empty chair.*)

Mother (*after a long silence*): I almost went. I felt uncomfortable and thought I'd go sit there.
Maria: I'm not comfortable here in the middle. Maybe I'd better take my other chair.
Father: It's your fisrt impulse that counts—and you took that chair.
Therapist (*to Giovanna*): When will someone in this family take an interest in you?

Giovanna: I don't know. Maybe I don't do anything to attract their attention.

Therapist: How many decades do you think it will take?

Mother: I helped her when she was sick . . . that's why I got sick,
later, when Antonio died.

Therapist: Blah, Blah, Blah! A person doesn't feel sick when they're
close to a sister or her fiance who is dying. That's healthy and normal. (*to Giovanna*) There's always someone in this family who
has a harder time than you; do you realize that? Why don't you
change seats to see how it feels once and for all . . . or do you (*to
Maria*) need to be the crazy one forever?

Maria: No sir, let her be the crazy one. And, look, I'm not crazy, just
desperate.

Therapist: I'd like to find out if, for once, Giovanna isn't even more
desperate.

Maria: She says no. I'm the star of the craziness script. It's not my fault.
I don't know why Giovanna wanted to come here. I don't know if
she was worried about me or about herself.

Therapist: That's our mystery! What do you think about it?

Maria: I think she's concerned about herself and I willingly give her
this chair. (*to Giovanna*) I give you this chair, if you want it, because I'm sick and tired of being leading lady. Will you take my
place?

Giovanna: I don't know. I think that when you're past 30, like me, you
don't have to be the center of attraction in the family.

Maria: So what did you hope to accomplish by coming here?

Giovanna: Above all, I guess, to talk about things we never would
talk about. At least to face each other. But I don't want the chair.
It's not for me. I want to resolve my problems in some other way. I
don't see why we always need an actress at the center of the family.

Franco: See, Giovanna, there's always somebody quicker than you to
grab the spotlight.

Giovanna: That's life!

Therapist (*raising his voice*): Oh! Exactly *because* that's how life is. In
life people's emotions carry very different importance. Here, if
Maria plays the "pagliacci," everybody stands around in awe but
if you (*to Giovanna*) have a feeling, it counts about as much as a

dog's. I agreed to see you today because I could imagine what it meant to you to have lost your most important relationship outside of your family . . . not because you couldn't get along but because of a death. . . . What does this mean to you at 34? I expected that we would be able to talk about this today . . . about real problems. That's why I feel cheated and deluded.

Franco: Truthfully, Giovanna was in a bad way. She suffered a lot.

Maria: Well, I think she reacted very well. She has a character that reacts well. Or maybe now I'm beginning to think that she, too, played a part, like me, for many years. I played the part of the loony and she just acted a different role.

Therapist: That's true. How did you play your part Giovanna?

Giovanna: How did I play my part? . . . I tried to speak openly with you, Maria. You had shared so much of my story with Antonio. So I said to you the situation is what it is; let's try to get over it. But it's very clear that deep inside me I haven't gotten over it. Then when mother came home did we ever talk about any of it? No! I kept everything inside pretending for your sakes that nothing was going on. That's the part I played and I didn't ask anybody to be upset by what had happened to me.

Mother: Do you really think that by keeping everything inside, we wouldn't feel it? Well, I felt it just the same even though you didn't say anything.

From the very beginning the therapist has received the message projected by the family: "There is an empty chair in the middle of our family circle." But what does it mean? The chair is for the person who feels the worst, he says, and immediately redefines in terms of suffering that which the family hastens to accept as illness. The therapist has uncovered Giovanna's suffering. He refuses to permit Maria to become the focus of attention once again. There is someone else who has a right to that focus. And Maria no longer has a reason to play the part of the "loony." By denying her this central role he gives her leeway to play a different role in the family. By pointing up the presence of very real pain he opens the way for everyone in the family to feel free to reach his or her own suffering.

CHAPTER 6

Metaphor and the Metaphoric Object in Therapy

METAPHORIC LANGUAGE

Metaphor abounds in everyday language where, by means of images based on similarity, it allows us to reproduce the reality and objects which surround us, in the same way that a map reproduces a territory. Unlike a map, however, the meaning of language and of its metaphoric images changes according to its context and according to the connotations that have been superimposed in the various circumstances in which these images have been used (Eco, 1975; Conte, 1981). As a result, at different times different characteristics of the object, situation or action to which the metaphor refers will assume greater importance, just as any object reveals different qualities when viewed under a ray of light that explores its surface from different angles.

92

This explains why metaphor so readily lends itself to use by family members in expressing states of mind or relational situations, as well as by the therapist in his effort to analyze and restructure the family system. Metaphor seems to spring from our need to stop the continuous flow of reality in order to possess it, to recapture what we lose of our everyday experience by means of something that resembles it. Even the symptom presented by a patient or a family can become a metaphor of a relational problem, an attempt to reconcile contradictory needs by means of a symbol capable of reflecting multiple meanings.*

Thus, a patient who isn't getting along with his mate, upon whom he is, however, dependent, may show that he cannot "swallow" certain elements in the union by vomiting. This symptom becomes the means for revealing the depth of exasperation while still allowing the dependence to be maintained. It is as though the metaphoric quality of the symptom were the agent for crystallizing and reconciling contrasting aspects of reality. In fact, if the symptom is not resolved, it may in time become the crossroad where situations originally remote from each other intersect. To return to the preceding example, the patient's vomiting may express his marital difficulties while also becoming a metaphor of problems in his relations with his family of origin. In this way a series of different memories become superimposed on one another and condensed in a single symbol. The symptom may now lose its specific character and become generalized, freed of time and space, valid in any circumstances. Only the patient's personal history determines when and where the symptomatic behavior will occur.

In general, by the time the therapist enters the scene, the evolution of the patient's "metaphor" has moved toward ever more abstraction and aspecificity. The therapist must, of necessity, initiate an opposing process, discovering within the images presented the original elements and

---

*This explains why we cannot solve the existential problem of an individual or family merely by uncovering a "traumatic" event or events and learning how it was experienced. In fact, the reevocation of an event occurs in a different context and is processed by a cognitive structure that assigns a different connotation to the event. For example, an adult in therapy who recalls the emotions associated with the trauma of separation from a parent is in a state that differs greatly from the original situation because of other factors that have intervened in his personal life. The significance he now attributes to the episode in question therefore represents the fruit of numerous interactions experienced by him which, through their repetition, have contributed to the development of his present cognitive structure.

relationships. He may also use his own metaphor to condense the observation he has made through the unfolding of the interaction among the members of the therapeutic system. The therapist may employ generic images, adaptable to numerous circumstances, but which nevertheless contain details perfectly applicable to the situation under scrutiny.

Let us examine how the metaphor may work when it is expressed by a patient through his symptom, as well as when it is used by the therapist. All of us use analogous mechanisms when the rules maintaining coherent social discourse are broken by our interlocutor. If, for example, (a) I (b) say something (c) to someone (d) in a specific situation, I may avoid defining the relationship by denying any single part or all four parts of the interaction. I may: (a) deny having *personally* communicated *something*; (b) deny that something *was communicated*; (c) deny that something was communicated to *the other person;* (d) deny *the context* in which it was communicated (Haley, 1963). This is valid for nonverbal as well as verbal messages, permitting acceptance at one level and denial at another.

It is clear that the patient with the symptom is not formally communicating any message, since his behavior is not voluntary; it is, therefore, "not he" who is communicating something. A structured communication is not explicitly established and it cannot, therefore, be formally considered as such, even more so if it is not openly directed to the person with whom the patient is interacting. For his part, when the therapist utilizes metaphor as his response to the patient, he proceeds in a like manner and his denial may concern one or more formal aspects of his message. *The metaphor is transmitted in the same mode in which the patient manifests the symptom, in a context and in a form which permits simultaneous affirmation and denial of both the content and the receiver of the message* (Bateson, 1972).

THE LITERARY METAPHOR

To clarify what we have been saying, let us examine the first session of a 15-year-old anorectic girl. Her parents, paternal grandmother, and other relatives of her father are present. Early in the session many disagreements between the parents surfaced, particularly a problem about the central role played by the paternal grandmother. The mother never felt accepted by her husband's family and perceived her position as marginal in the family structure. The birth of Carla, the anorectic patient, served to bring the parents closer together, creating a new family equilibrium. She has remained the "official" mediator of their rapport ever since.

Therapist (*to father*): So Carla helped to unite you with your wife and separate you at the same time. What you weren't able to do for your wife you were able to do for your daughter?

Father: In a certain sense it was like that.

Therapist (*to the patient*): You, young lady . . . I can't quite understand why this lovely young lady felt so grandiose, so . . . Do you know Don Quixote? Don Quixote believed he was always the victor; in every situation, there he was in the middle . . . but at the end he was just a poor devil who got beaten left and right . . . apparently a caricature, but really someone who . . . he didn't even know who he was. No? Do you agree with me?

Carla: I have to . . .

Therapist (*interrupting*): He was a bit like you. He looked like you; he had this (*indicating the patient's body*); he was always perfectly dressed; he had his sword, his shield. . . . Well, you have a beautiful purse, your fancy boots . . . but I have a feeling that inside you're sort of like Don Quixote because you've got it into your head to win like he did. You think you can take on all the tensions, all the problems . . . you think that they (*indicating the parents*) can't manage. The anger and hate that your mother nurtures which she must always deny, however . . . you've taken the hatred, the blackmail, and something else which isn't yet clear to me and you've decided to direct all the traffic . . . well it's a grand gesture, but certainly . . .

Carla: I don't know if I did that, but if I did . . . for me . . . I did it unconsciously.

Therapist: Hm, with this "unconsciously" the story doesn't change much . . . also because even if you didn't know what you were doing initially, you're perfectly conscious of what you're doing now. (*Carla trys to interrupt but her father shushes her.*) . . .

> You know only too well that your mother was never accepted, that she feels that whatever recognition she's gotten was because of you and not because of her and maybe sometimes she thought it would have been better if you hadn't ever been . . .

(Carla bursts into tears)

Therapist: The only difference is that Don Quixote never cried and this gives me some hope. If you can cry it means that . . . well, you may not end up the same way.

An analysis of this segment shows that, using the image of Don Quixote, the therapist was able to embody a series of the patient's behaviors and functions while relating the connotations which characterize this literary personage and which represent the terms of their familial confrontation. Carla, therefore, no longer must seek a definition of herself in a reality and in relationships in constant flux, since these have been disclosed and fixed for her in an image which contains a definition and a history, an image which compares elements "external" to the patient herself.

This is a most important point because one of the major problems each of us meets in our own evolution and in our efforts to change is the problem of being able to *separate from ourselves* and face our true image. Change can only be triggered by such a confrontation, by the assessment of the difference between one state and another, by an interruption and an arbitrary punctuation in the continuous flow of experience.

The image used defines not only the identified member of the family but also the relationships and interactions which he or she has with the others, all occurring in an unreal and fantastic atmosphere. Even though the metaphoric message is ostensibly directed at only one person, its structure indirectly involves the others to the degree in which they relate to him. It is as if they were told, "The moment that you accept an exchange with (in this instance) Carla, you enter into a land of make-believe." Once again, this world loses its specific temporal and spatial qualities, while retaining the universal attributes linked with the literary figure. This last fact is what establishes the framework for successive exchanges.

Details and their place in time and space will be supplied by Carla's place in the ongoing family history, by the way she defines each participant and by the way she sees her own actions.

The worlds of literature and the theater constantly give us examples paralleling this procedure when they present us with classical figures who are equally viable in contemporary dramas.

THE CONTEXTUAL METAPHOR

The use of metaphor goes beyond the aforementioned situation wherein the therapist makes explicit reference to the connection between the person and the metaphoric image. In other instances it is used with much more subtlety; the therapist picks up on and amplifies even a single, "casual" comment with metaphoric overtones which the patient may use. This comment might pass unobserved if the therapist did not expand on it to such a point that it moves beyond being a subject for discussion and becomes an actual *contextual framework*. We will see this more clearly and in more detail when we examine the metaphoric object.

There are other times when the therapist may condense into one metaphor many factors derived from observations he has made of the family transactions, arranging it so that the final definition of the metaphor is made by the patient, as we shall see in the following example.

On the appointed day the patient appeared with the members of her family: her first and second husbands (her first husband still managed the family's finances), and her daughters from both marriages. She was still an attractive woman, meticulously dressed and made up despite her "depression." Her way of moving and speaking conveyed her claim to being the center of all attention. She wore a turban and brandished a long cigarette-holder, final touches to her image as a "femme fatale." The two husbands had an unassuming and detached air, as though they just happened to be there by chance. The daughters looked like poor little orphans in search of a refuge. The general atmosphere sug-

gested a group of people who had fallen under the curse of some malign
fate.

Therapist (*while entering, before sitting down*): Would you mind
    clearing off one of those two armchairs for mother? (*pointing to
    two armchairs in a corner on which personal belongings have
    been piled up*) (*to the patient*) Madame, would you please sit
    there? (*to the others*) Now, can you close the circle and forget
    about Tiziana? After all, you realize there's no hope in that direc-
    tion (*indicating Tiziana in the corner armchair*). This meeting
    will be useless unless all of you, or some of you, can escape from
    the curse. Or have you already given up hope? All of you?
First husband (*showing surprise*): I don't understand.
Therapist: I mean, is there any hope for the rest of you? Who has more
    hope? Who has less?
Giulia (*age 27, oldest daughter from the first marriage, in a funereal
    tone*): I think that each of us is looking for a way to live well.
Therapist: Yes, I can understand what you are looking for, but what
    you have found is a different matter.
Giulia: I think all of us are looking for something . . .
Therapist: Have you escaped from the curse, for example?
Giulia: What curse do you mean? This . . . this suffering because of
    things in the family? . . . No, I haven't escaped, I really haven't.
Therapist: Are you the one most imprisoned by the curse?
Giulia: Well, I'm certainly suffering from it. There are lots of things
    that can happen now that may have consequences later on. For
    example, she is the youngest. (*She indicates Sabina, the youngest
    daughter, who is 11.*)
Therapist: You mean she may be damaged by the curse even at a dis-
    tance?
Giulia: I dont' know; she has probably been damaged already, or she
    may suffer more later on. I feel responsible for her too, in some
    ways. She's still a child . . .
Therapist: Is it the curse that makes you play mother to Sabina?
Giulia: It's not that I play mother . . . sometimes I worry about a lot
    of things that happen to her, apart from what troubles me person-
    ally.

Therapist: Have you no children?

Giulia: No, I don't . . . I don't . . . think I want any because I wouldn't be capable . . . of . . . I wouldn't be calm enough, I wouldn't have anything positive to offer to children.

Therapist: So the curse has gotten to your uterus. (*turning to Grazia, the firstborn of the second marriage*) And what about you? Have you more hope or less hope of escaping from the curse?

Grazia: More or less like her (*turning toward Giulia*).

Therapist: So you won't have children either?

Grazia: Oh, definitely not!

Therapist: For how long have you been under the curse?

Grazia: (*with a mixture of anger and resignation*): Well, I think I always have been, or almost . . . well, I can't say exactly.

As we see, the therapist has made his interlocutors look at themselves vis-à-vis the image he gave them (the curse). More and more the particulars become defined, taking on greater personal connotations as the responses are made. At the moment when each one accepts the metaphor it becomes the core of the discussion and every affirmation is implicitly linked to it. *The therapist traces out the patterns of the associations while the family provides the material.*

Two disparate perceptive worlds blend together in this process: that of the therapist and that of the family. The product of this integration becomes part of the culture of the therapeutic system and therefore functions as an important factor in the associations among all the elements within the system. In the preceding example this kind of assimilation into the common cultural baggage was demonstrated when one of the family members spontaneously used the same image previously offered by the therapist.

At times the therapist may use metaphors continuously, arriving, ultimately, at an allegorical discussion. Here, the connection with the real subject of the discussion is established only through the context wherein the dialogue unfolds. The therapist may relate fantasies which come to mind or anecdotes about other patients, but he seeks to avoid connecting these with the persons directly interested, anticipating their possible objections. He may use phrases such as: "But I'm not referring to you" or "Evidently this doesn't mean you."

The idea of the comparison is implicitly planted, even if it is formally denied, as we shall see in the next case, where the family is asked to create a fairy tale with clear reference to its problem. Such a procedure is justified by the age of the identified patient, Marco, a five-year-old in therapy for problems with his sexual identity. The objective of the session was to clarify and make explicit the relationship between the function of Marco's symptom and the function of his parents in a climate wherein they might express the conflicts surrounding their own sexuality. It was necessary to answer the question: Who has the penis in the family, father or mother?

Therapist (*entering*): Now let's play together. Take away the chairs and let's sit on the floor. (*Everyone sits on the floor, laughing.*) Let's do it this way: The grown-ups tell a fairy tale to the kids. . . . I'll begin.
Mother: Who will be next?
Therapist: You all choose. . . . Okay? Once upon a time there was a little boy who couldn't tell very well whether his father had a penis or if his mother had it. . . . Who will go next, mother or dad?
Mother: Marco, you must listen.
Father (*to Marco*): Well . . . this little boy who didn't know what his father had, what do you suppose he did in order to find out? He said to himself: "If I go look when my father gets undressed, I'll know. But if I want to know without seeing him undressed, what can I do?
Therapist: Will mother take over?
Marco: I'll do it. I already know; it's a penis!
Mother: Who has it?
Marco: Daddy has it! Daddy has it!
Mother: Well, this little boy, because he didn't know, went and put on his mother's clothes *and* his father's clothes, but he put his father's on underneath and his mother's on the outside.
Marco: No!
Therapist: He was so smart when he put his mother's clothes on with his father's underneath that he was able to confuse everybody. He also knew that if he wanted to please everybody it was better to wear both the skirt and the pants.

Father: That I don't know, but since he wears both the skirt and the
      pants he can play a man when it's convenient and a lady when it
      suits him as well. Am I right?
Therapist: And how.

THE METAPHORIC OBJECT:
THE THERAPIST'S "INVENTION"

One of the characteristics of the use of metaphor is that it enables
one to create an image of the emotions of a person's behavior, of his
character, or of his relationships within a system. The representations
possible are practically infinite, but here we are interested in exploring
only a few.

We speak of "objects" because every representation is a "photo-
graph" of reality, its arbitrary crystallization. This offers us the advantage of viewing the representations as observable elements outside of
the flow of what is actually happening. We can, however, compare
them in a series of processes otherwise indefinable in order to make
them "real" and fixed in time.

In the course of a session the therapist may choose material objects
which seem most suitable for representing behavior, relationships, interactions, or the rules of the family involved in treatment. He must
then pay particular attention to the interactions of family and the therapist and to the communicative redundancy shown there, seeing himself in the middle of it all, with his way of acting, his personality, and
his emotional makeup.

The choice of the metaphoric object is an inventive act by the therapist with which he introduces a new "code" which defines and interprets what is happening. This code forms the basis for redefining the
relationship among the family members and between them and the
therapist (Angelo, 1981).

Here is an example from the same session with Carlo which was
used earlier in Chapter 3. We are in a later part of the session, still an-
alyzing Carlo's mother's function and the way she meshes with the
other family members. Someone has just suggested that she, the mother, is perhaps the "keystone" for understanding the family situation.
The therapist immediately picks up on this metaphoric image.

Therapist (*to mother*): I don't know. In which lock does the key turn? What doors does it open; what doors does it keep locked? What are the right slots? . . . If you could talk about yourself how would you describe your doors and your keys? . . .

Mother: I must say all in all I'm a woman who lives pretty much . . . with her feet on the ground in practical matters . . .

Therapist: But the keys . . .

Mother: Oh, yes, in what sense?

Therapist: Everyone has keys, no? . . . To the house, to the car . . .

Mother: Hmm, yes . . .

Therapist: There are the keys to the front door, keys to the bedroom if you want to keep it locked, the keys to the closet . . .

Mother: Right, lots of different keys . . .

Therapist (*continuing*): You could give or not give the keys to the others. . . . Do you understand the question now?

Mother: What's my role, in other words . . .

Therapist: Yes, what do you open and what do you lock?

Mother: I'm the manager of the keys. (*laughing*)

Therapist: Which ones?

Mother: The keys to the house.

Therapist: Yes, but I don't know the house. It might have 20 rooms, or two . . . I don't know. Or maybe some keys are more important than others . . .

Mother: Give me a key hook, then, no . . . (*They all laugh.*)

Father: The key is figurative.

Therapist: You want a hook. . . . Do you have a bunch of keys in your purse?

Mother: Yes . . . (*digging in her purse she takes out a bunch of keys*).

Therapist: Why don't you give out some of these keys. . . . Give some to the others and tell them which rooms they open. Keep the ones you are certain are yours and give the others the remaining ones. Don't give any to the ones who don't need any.

Mother (*taking out the keys and handing them out, speaking in a loud voice*): I'm keeping the keys to the kitchen without a doubt—nobody would take those from me . . . (*laughter*). The living room keys are half for me and half for my son (*the older son*) who doesn't allow anyone in a certain part of the room. . . .

Therapist: Okay. Then give half the living room to Gianni.
Mother (*proceeding*): To this gentleman (*indicating the patient*) I give
    the key to my bedroom, because he is really the proprietor of it
    . . . to my husband I don't know what to give really because . . .
Father: I'm left out . . . (*giggles*).
Mother: Oh, yes, he has a study, a study that's a mess. I can't even step
    into it, it makes my hair stand on end.
Therapist: Who doesn't like his key and would like a different one?
Father: Me! Hm . . . the key that I don't have anymore . . . I want
    it. . . .
Therapist: Which key do you want?
Father: The one to the bedroom.
Therapist: See if you can get it.
Father: He's got to give it to me (*pointing to the patient*).
Therapist: If you take it.

This segment demonstrates how an image expressed by one of the participants in the session may serve as the pivotal element for developing the intervention. The advantage to using a metaphor coming directly from the family lies in the fact that it reduces the possibilities for resistance. It is difficult to deny an image which already forms part of their perceptive and symbolic heritage. At this point, however, it is not only their perception which is involved but also the therapist's perception, together with his creativity. The session thus becomes the *setting where two different worlds meet* (Nicolò, 1980). In addition to serving as an important element in the relationship, the metaphor becomes the point of departure for a circularity in which each response to the image raised by the therapist or his interlocutor gives rise to the stimulation of new, related images.

Here, the metaphor is given substance through selecting the mother's keys, which reinforces not just the image but also its significance within the family. The mother's keys embody the relationships, the habits, and the rules existing in their group.

Using the metaphoric object rather than merely metaphor, the therapist may more effectively *withdraw from the center*. He no longer is the focus of attention, the reference point for the group. The focal point becomes that object, that material element, which gets passed from one to the other, weighed and examined, as if it held a deep secret to be decoded (Angelo, 1981).

We have been struck by the similarity between the use of the metaphoric object and the implements used by witch doctors in their healing rites, wherein they dispatch the malady, transforming it into a concrete image.

The object may be extremely effective when a situation becomes confused or bogs down in an impasse. Using the metaphoric object, the therapist is able to "throw the ball" back to the family and to observe what happens from the sidelines. At the same time it provides him with a solid *point of reference* to which he may return at the end of every interactive digression (Angelo, 1981).

The metaphoric object, even more than metaphor, presents many levels for changing connections. The clear visual and tactile presence accentuates the contrast between its literal, material meaning and its symbolic implications, creating confusion as to which level is relevant to the message received. Since the one receiving the message may also speak of elements important in his relationships, he feels both stimulated to examine these relationships and free to gauge their intensity.

This becomes particularly evident when puppets are used as the object. It is most important that the representative object holds both a very precise and a very vague reference. An object will be proportionately more effective if it evokes certain details relevant to the relationships or persons involved *and* an ambiguous and general context as well. This increases stress and confusion, which are indispensable for seeking alternative behavior and meaning.

THE METAPHORIC OBJECT: THE ELEMENT OF DRAMATIZATION

The fact that the metaphor may find its material support in the metaphoric object permits us to use it to dramatize the relationships within the system. This may come about through direct dialogue, if puppets or an object which represents a person are used, or through passing the object from one person to another, where the *action* itself takes on symbolic significance. The object serves as the receiver and carrier of all the connotations implied by each person, including the therapist.

In the following segment with Carla (see p. 95), the therapist enters the session with a ball which is weighted inside with sand so that its trajectory is unpredictable. In fact, stamped upon it is the name "crazy ball."

Therapist (*just entering the session, turning to Carla, the patient, pointing to the ball he is carrying*): This is you!

Carla (*looking at the ball, speaking in a quiet voice*): Beautiful!

Therapist: I brought it just for that reason. But it's a special ball. . . . Do you know why it's special?

Carla: No!

Therapist (*extending the ball toward her*): Do you want to see it? Want to try it?

Carla: No!

Father (*turned toward Carla*): Aren't you curious about it?

Carla: I don't want it!

Therapist: Somebody here must be curious. (*turning to father*) You are curious to know what's like your daughter (*giving him the ball*).

Father (*turning the ball around in a puzzled manner and reading what is written on it*): I know what "crazy" means so this is called "crazy ball."

Therapist: I'm beginning to think that you're a bit like your daughter.

Father: Well, I don't see any similarity.

Therapist: Could you throw it to your daughter? Then maybe you two will understand. . . . Throw it!

Father (*to his daughter, after having thrown the ball in a bizarre trajectory. He speaks jokingly*): There, see? That was quite a strange path . . . no? If you go around with a ball like that everyone will take you for Pele. . . . Pele did those tricks with a normal ball! . . .

Therapist: And you (*looking at Carla*), do you manage to make a normal ball do crazy things?

Carla: Why is it like me?

Therapist: Don't you know?

Carla: No.

Therapist: You always want to play the jester. You're not really a jester, you know?

Father (*to Carla*): Are you beginning to see how it resembles you?

Carla: That it acts strangely?

Father: Why? Do you act strangely?

Carla: Because the ball isn't a normal ball. It does different things, things that you don't expect . . . I don't know . . .

Therapist (*to mother*): And you, mother, . . . can you help us?

Mother: I'm thinking . . .

Therapist: Okay. If you take hold of it . . . (*the mother takes the ball and seems perplexed by it*). Maybe you should all use it a bit . . . maybe it will come a little more easily. Why don't you throw it to your husband or your daughter? Some idea or image will strike you. . . . There's lots of room here, play ball any way you wish. (*The members of the family begin to play ball among themselves. When they throw it, it almost always goes off course.*)

Carla (*at the end, to the therapist*): Maybe it's because, unlike other balls, this one goes where *it* wants and not where you expect it to go . . .

Therapist: You don't have to convince me. Talk it over with your parents.

Carla: I don't know . . . I want to ask you if that's so . . .

Therapist: I asked you for answers, not for questions!

Mother: The only thing I can think of is that this is a most unusual ball, different from all the others, and it reacts in a different way. . . . There, that's surely like Carla and the way she behaves . . . maybe she often reacted to problems, to things . . . in ways that were very different from how people should react.

Carla (*to the therapist*): Does this ball have something inside that makes it move that way?

Father: Try it; listen! (*Carla does as he says and shakes the ball*).

Carla: Is it another ball? And I have something inside of me, too, that makes me act strangely?

Father: In what sense?

Carla: Well, I don't know . . . the ball . . . it's in charge of the game . . . and I think I'm grown-up and can do everything alone, but I'm really kidding myself. . . .

Father: According to that, it would seem as if she's in charge of the game and that we fool ourselves with her. . . .

This fragment introduces a new dimension in the use of the metaphoric object and the metaphor in general. After the initial comparison between the crazy ball and the patient and the first attempts at interpretation, the therapist asks the family to get involved in an exchange. In this exchange, the "bizarre" object serves both as the stimulus for the action and the key to its own significance. Each one has the chance to act on his or her relationship with the patient, and, through her, with the others as well, as participant and observer. Often this leads to a turning point in terms of their vision of reality. The father's final words support this clearly, " . . . it would seem as if she's in charge of the game and that we fool ourselves with her"

Once again, we see that through the amplification of one of the characteristics of the function of the identified patient, dimensions were perceived which made interrelated situations appear equally distorted.

THE METAPHORIC OBJECT:
A FAMILY "INVENTION"

Another way of employing the object in therapy is to use the object or objects which the family brings to the session. Initially these hold a significance for the family members different from that which the therapist attributes to these objects. In daily life, within the various systems in which we participate, each of us is surrounded by objects which help define the context for our interactions and qualify the characteristics of the persons who use them. Objects may, therefore, be consciously used as instruments of communication (Miller, 1978).

The following example is taken from therapy with a family having two obese children, Paolo, 12, and Franca, 10. The children appear at the session with a bag of fruit which they are enthusiastically eating, taking no notice of anyone else present but holding the center of general attention. The father is sitting slightly to one side, while the grandmother seems very close to the mother. The whole picture connotes an inversion of roles between parents and children. The therapist decides to underscore this.

Father: Children are children and not parents . . .
Therapist: That depends. It looks like he (*nodding toward Paolo*) acts

like a parent because he provides food for everyone.

Father: You're right. He's always stuffing himself. Eating . . . eating . . . he's like a horse.

Therapist: Don't you ever think about giving your father something to eat too?

Father: Look, that stuff doesn't go with me. I don't eat; I'm not insatiable. He can do whatever he wants, but I stay like this.

Therapist (*to Paolo*): Did you ever consider giving someone else the last thing you have to eat? (*Paolo is holding a banana. At the question, Paolo offers the banana to his mother.*)

Mother (*slightly annoyed*): No, I'm not hungry; I can't . . .

Father (*to the son, pointing to the banana*): Take it home; take it home . . .

Therapist: Well, then, the problem for you people here is that the adults don't want the kids' food.

Mother: The problem is a different one. We're here because our children eat like horses and when we go out people laugh at us because they're so fat . . .

Therapist: It's true. How can the children lose weight if they have to eat all the food since the parents don't eat it. (*to father*) Can't you even have a small piece of banana?

Father: Do I have to have it now?

Therapist: Yes.

Mother: Did we come here to have a snack? (*laughing*)

Therapist: I'd like to understand. What would happen to the kids if father would eat a piece of banana? Maybe they're afraid he might choke if he ate it . . .

Mother (*smiling*): I think you're making us look ridiculous.

Therapist: Well, we all have our ridiculous sides, but maybe you're right . . . but what really does seem ridiculous to me is that in this family only the children eat; the adults, no.

In this case the therapist uses the food brought to the session by the children and referred to by the parents in their definition of the problem (their children's obesity). The therapist redefines its significance and gives it a metaphoric value. The food becomes the mediator for family relationships; the feelings within these relationships, as well as the possibilities for exchanges, are examined. Pointing out the inversion of familial hierarchy allows the therapist to move the focus of attention to problems other than the ones initially advanced. By alluding to these, the therapist makes it harder for the family to raise objections later on.

Tradition and culture offer us the possibility of associating food with other elements in our relationships (sexual relationships, affective exchanges, power struggles, etc.). A dialogue with many referents may be conducted without the need to ask embarrassing questions. In this sense, the food-object becomes a real and true *qualifier of messages*.

We notice many elements of play in the use of metaphor and the metaphoric object, just as we can perhaps in every form of therapy (Bateson, 1972; Andolfi, 1979; Keith & Whitaker, 1981). It is difficult to determine up to what point play is important for each one of us, but it is certain that in the course of our lives each one of us must continually pass through one "game" or another to reach an equilibrium with the people in our lives and in our relation with reality. In childhood we play with our peers, recreating life situations, trying to interpret roles corresponding to the ideals passed to us by the adults in our lives. We test reality in a paradoxical way through our play, performing "acts" of reality in a context which, however, denies their reality. The objects we use in our play take on multiple characteristics because they both "are and are not" what they represent. This allows each of us to test his or her vision of the world and relationships with others in a fictional situation, which nevertheless may be transposed in large part to reality where the distinction between one plane and another is made to a great extent by contextual elements.

These situations are constantly repeated in our day-to-day adult existence, where the meaning of what is said and done is often implicit or even denied. If we are discussing something of importance to us and we wish to "better understand" the other person, we may assume a joking attitude or make a light comment and wait for his reaction before deciding what tack to take. Should we be allusive or serious? Should we deny what was just said by saying "I was only kidding," or should we admit our real intentions, our real sentiments? With our partner-in-dialogue we construct a game in which we clearly delineate the points of reference. It is a way to take stock of the relative value of what is happening and to end up "laughing" over what is "serious" or, at least, "should be" serious. Self-irony and the ability to laugh at yourself indicate the ability to size yourself up, accepting your inevitable contradictions and finding the bases for transcending them.

It is rather easy to see how the bizarre elements and the humor in the cases reported can become aids to gaining greater knowledge. If reality and the tragic sense which often accompanies it can be transformed into play, it may be possible to dissolve the connections among the stereotypical functions of each member of the system, and to free the creative potential inherent in the family.

CHAPTER 7

The Fraioli Family:
A Case History

The case of a family whose identified patient was schizophrenic illustrates what we have presented so far. We saw this family fortnightly for 23 sessions.

The Fraioli family came to us after years of fruitless, repeated interventions of different schools of treatment. This middle-class nuclear family was from a small city in Northern Italy. The stern father, a doctor, was a rigid Catholic with many sexual phobias. The mother, apparently a committed housewife, subtly managed to play a dominating role in the family organization. Father was 13 years older than the mother. They had four children, three sons and then a daughter rather late in life. The girl of 22 lived outside of the home, as did the two eldest brothers, aged 36 and 34. The third son, Giuseppe, the identified patient, was the only child living with the parents.

Giuseppe, 28, after isolating himself more and more over the past few years, has now reached the point where he never leaves the house.

The authors are grateful to Katia Giacometti for her editing of this chapter.

His depression, aggressive behavior at home, and progressive distancing from external reality have culminated in worrisome episodes of psychomotor agitation, religious and sexual fantasies, and even in serious attempts at suicide. Despite a brilliantly earned degree in law he has given up any hope of working and spends his time either in his room or lolling about the house haunted by fantasies of sex and death. He masturbates openly, using his mother's underclothes for self-excitation. He also has openly expressed his desire to have sexual relations with her.

His designation as patient is of long standing and is supported by a heavy dossier covering various types of psychotherapy (from psychopharmacological to psychoanalytical), conducted by well-known professionals. Despite this, Guiseppe has had several hospitalizations. His illness has dominated family life for some time, resulting in his receiving the constant attention of the mother and moralistic lectures from the father.

INTERVENTION: A DESTABILIZING PROCESS

Ten minutes of the first session have passed with father, mother, and Giuseppe present. Giuseppe, seated between his parents, appears very tense and stares at the floor with an expressionless gaze while his parents talk about him.

Mother: He's next to the youngest. The eldest is 36 and he's a lawyer in LaSpezia. Our second son is 34 and he works in a bank in Parma. Our daughter, the youngest . . .

Father (*interrupting his wife*): . . . Well he has excellent possibilities but . . . now you'll learn what his problems are . . . that's why he's lost his way . . . we're ready to make any sacrifice . . . you know, it's a hard cross to bear, seeing a son reduced to this . . .

The father puts Giuseppe right in the center. As his parents discuss him, he appears to visibly shrink, almost reducing his physical space.

Mother (*interrupting*): I had been
hoping to have a girl . . . but he
was the third boy. . . . He had a
more docile, sweeter character
than the other boys so I kept him
rather close to me . . . and he
seemed to prefer that too. . . .
We spent vacations together, for
example . . . something the older boys almost never did . . .

Father (*speaking simultaneously
with her*): It's not that we think
he's the black sheep. . . . Look, I
am a good enough Christian to
say what needs saying: "Dear
Jesus, whatever God in Heaven
wills us. . . . " He sent me a son
like this and I keep him, try to
help him, and he stubbornly refuses my help.

Therapist (*to the father*): I'd like to   The therapist interprets Giuseppe's
find out how Giuseppe is feeling   nonverbal messages and makes
because I would feel very un-   them explicit. He reads his behav-
comfortable in his place.   ior, which in other contexts is con-
    sidered inappropriate, as a manifes-
    tation of a plausible state of mind.
    He shows that he is interested in
    the patient as a person and not only
    in his symptomatic behavior. He
    accepts the centrality of Giuseppe
    in this way. But in respect to the
    expectations of the system, he asso-
    ciates himself with Giuseppe in an
    unpredictable way.

Giuseppe: I don't feel at all uncomfortable . . . (*muttering discon-
nectedly*).

Therapist: Right now you look ex-   The accent is on how the patient's
tremely uncomfortable . . . even   physical space has been noticeably
the way you're sitting . . .   reduced, invaded by the verbal and
    emotional space of his parents.

Giuseppe: Now I'm pissed off.

Therapist: Hmm . . . let's say you're pissed off . . . about being here?

> The therapist binds himself with the patient's emotional state, introducing an element of definition outside of the system.

Giuseppe (*more decidedly*): No, I'm pissed off because of my goddamned tricks.* I don't need sympathy from anyone, I don't need any help with my damn tricks, I can manage perfectly well by myself.

> The patient's response to the therapist is clearly provocative. The mother and father appear worried, grieved, and resigned to their role as parents of a mentally ill son. In this way the family challenges the therapist to face up to a lost cause.

Therapist: Give me an example of what you mean by "tricks," because maybe the way we use the word in Rome is different from the way it's used where you lived. . . . Maybe you don't mean what I am thinking of.

> The therapist does not retreat from Giuseppe's linguistic assault; on the contrary, he calls attention to it and uses it himself. The way that the therapist calmly repeats and analyzes Giuseppe's words gives his behavior a connotation of normality.

The therapist accepts the system's challenge and he used the centrality of the patient to introduce a new point: The patient is so very important because in a "logical" and "voluntary" way he performs actions which are "essential" to the functioning of the family.

Giuseppe (*provocatively*): I want a woman so I can shove it up her ass, but I've never done anything.

> The patient calls attention back to himself by using provocative means.

Therapist: You want to . . . ?

Giuseppe: Shove it up her ass . . . but I've never done anything . . .

Therapist: Do you mean you've never shoved it up a woman's

> The therapist insists on concrete, specific answers, which makes Giu-

---

* *Translator's note:* Giuseppe uses the slang expression "puttanata," from "puttana" ("prostitute"). A puttanata is something unworthy; it also has the connotation of a "gyp."

ass, or you've never had sexual relations of any kind?

Giuseppe: I've had some sexual relations . . . but only using certain methods. Anyway, only with hookers.

Therapist: Well, they are more willing, aren't they? What is the problem? I mean about shoving it . . .

Giuseppe (*surprised*): What did you say?

Therapist: I mean hookers really are more willing, aren't they? They have a more easygoing attitude toward their own bodies. Did you have any problems with them?

Giuseppe: No.

Therapist: I don't see where the tricks are, except in the literal sense of turning a trick with a hooker. I still don't understand what you mean. Can you explain it better?

Giuseppe: I'm ashamed, so I get inhibited. I always get inhibited . . .

Therapist: You mean you get inhibited about shoving it up a woman's ass or about having sexual relations in general? That's not clear to me.

seppe's statements seem less eccentric. It also deprives the patient of power and reduces the sense of drama in the session.

The therapist's implicit redefinition of Giuseppe's behavior as normal constitutes a counterprovocation of the identified patient and his family. Giuseppe responds with surprise. What we might call "the caricature of pathology" begins to come into play here. The use of humor, which we will see in other passages, tends to relieve the sense of drama in the context and to create a certain distance vis-à-vis the problem.

Giuseppe: This year, and maybe
even last year, too, I made pro-
posals to a few women, but I
never got anywhere.
Therapist: Okay, but I still don't
know what you mean by your
damn tricks.
Mother (*ingratiatingly*): May I . . .
Therapist: (*to Giuseppe*): You told
me that you are pissed off because of your goddamned tricks.
I think there are lots of young
men your age who would like to
take a woman and shove it up
her ass. . . . I don't know what
seems so extraordinary to you.
Maybe you want some very special kind of ass . . . maybe that's
what makes you feel bad . . .
Giuseppe: I think it's something
I'll never be able to obtain . . .
Therapist: From yourself or from
a woman?
Giuseppe: What did you say?
Therapist: From yourself or from
a woman?

Giuseppe: From women.
Therapist: Are you sure?
Giuseppe: I think so.
Therapist: Because from the way
you talk, it sounds as though
you have some problems of your
own.

Depriving Giuseppe of the family's
support enables him to explore
other personal areas.

The initiative is now firmly in
the hands of the therapist. He en-
courages the patient to confront
him directly.

The context is now completely appropriate. The difference between
the "patient" and the other participants is losing all significance. Giuseppe's answers all are fitting.

The therapist constantly picks up
from the nonverbal aspects of the
patient his true suffering despite his
provocative verbalizations.

At this point the father and mother intervene, trying to convince the
therapist that Giuseppe's behavior is really very seriously disturbed.
The therapist responds:

Therapist: I really don't understand. . . . You have taken a long trip by train, you even had to sleep in Rome last night in order to come here today. . . . If the problem is just shoving it up someone's ass, I can't see why the situation is so serious.

Father: But he has tried to commit suicide because of that . . .

Therapist: Yes, I know, but so far I have no idea of how that all happened. It doesn't seem to be a problem that deserves so much attention and so many doctors . . .

The therapist explicitly denies that the identified patient is mentally ill and implicitly communicates that he is not willing to play with the rules of the relationship which maintain the status quo. He is ready to enter the system but at another level.

The parents now start relating a series of episodes to support their conviction that Giuseppe is in fact very ill. The therapist interrupts them and again resumes his provocation of Giuseppe. It is not important, in fact, to gather information from a mass of confused ideas and facts which may or may not be relevant. What is important is to be open to perceiving those elements (verbal and, above all, nonverbal) that reflect the conflict between the need for differentiation and the need for cohesion, elements that represent the attempt to fuse contradictory aspects of the same reality (Andolfi & Angelo, 1981). By interrupting the parents and resuming his provocation of Giuseppe, the therapist achieves his objective of disturbing the scenario worked out by the family. He then can proceed toward the formation of a therapeutic system which uses an "input" capable of keeping the expectations of the family system off balance (Andolfi et al., 1980). Any attempt at manipulation of the therapist by using the symptom is thereby eliminated.

Therapist: Would you please wait a moment, Mrs. Fraioli, because Giuseppe is still pissed off and I can't work with a family with a son who is how old? (*to Giuseppe*)

The therapist blocks the parents' attempt to reinstate Giuseppe as "the patient." At the same time he focuses the family's attention upon himself, clearing an open space which contradicts their stereotype

Giuseppe: 28.

Therapist: 28 years old. If you were only ten, I could accept your sitting here in silence and looking pissed off while your parents talk about you. But since you're 28, I can't accept it . . . so either we have to end this meeting or talk about why you are pissed off.

Giuseppe: I'm in this mood because . . .

Therapist: Perhaps I should explain this to you better: A person can be depressed, or worried, or sad — but if he's pissed off, he certainly won't cooperate. Do you see what I mean? That's what worries me . . . if you're pissed off, you won't be able to help us. If your mother or father or I . . . if any of us were pissed off, we wouldn't be able to help. So if we don't deal with the fact that you are pissed off, I can't go on. I even had to interrupt your mother who was trying to tell me what happened in 1972. . . . Maybe you are pissed off at me . . .

Giuseppe (animatedly): Yes, as a matter of fact, while I was waiting to come over here, I was saying, "Now I have to go to see that pain-in-the-ass."

of the expected therapeutic session.

Since the therapist refuses to let the patient continue playing the role of the sick member who needs protection, he cannot accept the patient's silence. He therefore defines Giuseppe's silence (and all of his other behaviors in the sessions) as voluntary. The plan is: attack the symptom (along with the dysfunctional organization of the system) but support the person. This will be a constant throughout the therapy.

It is a clear message to Giuseppe and the rest of the family: "The collaboration of everyone is necessary here." The therapist changes his position as outside observer and participating member. By accentuating Giuseppe's relationship with him he is able to move the pathology from the individual to his relationships (Andolfi, 1979). He offers himself as a point of reference around which the family must seek a new organization. One of the new rules is that each one must see himself as an active and participating element in the system. The process of differentiation of each one, in fact, begins in the relationship with the therapist.

Giuseppe returns the provocation . . .

Therapist: I'm glad you call a spade a spade. I like that; you are frank.

. . . and the therapist redefines it in a positive sense. He challenges the rule of the system which sacrifices every individual manifestation of emotion to an undifferentiated familial emotion (Bowen, 1978).

Giuseppe: Of course, since . . .

Therapist: But I want to know just one thing. Why are you pissed off, here, today?

The therapist again invites the identified patient to deal directly with a concrete issue. His refusal to be an agent for change is paralleled with an action of differentiation revolving around him which avoids openly challenging the intrafamilial equilibrium.

Giuseppe: You want to know what's bugging me?

Therapist: Yes, precisely.

Giuseppe: Because by now this situation has become a tremendous nuisance, I'm fed up, I'm pissed off, I'm furious. For example, I'm continually bugging my parents . . . but naturally I don't do the same thing to my brothers and sister because they would think I was nuts . . . so I don't do it to them.

Therapist: Just a minute, I understood everything up to a certain point, but then I couldn't follow you anymore . . . because in my opinion it's not that they would think you were nuts — but that they would tell you to shove it up your ass.

By surpassing the patient's own use of provocative language, the therapist implicitly defines Giuseppe's behavior as appropriate. We begin to notice a difference between the parents' protective attitude, based on the premise that Giuseppe is mentally ill, and the reactive behavior of his siblings, based on the assumption that Giuseppe's behavior is voluntary and responsible.

Giuseppe: You are right.

Therapist: That's different from thinking that you're nuts.

Giuseppe: They would think I was nuts, and they would also tell me to shove it.

Therapist: No, I think that they would tell you to shove it because they don't like to consider you nuts. It's a completely different story with your parents. They protect you because they're worried and they're afraid that you are nuts—so they think they can't tell you to shove it.

Giuseppe: What did you just say? My parents are afraid that . . .

Therapist: Basically, your parents are worried because they think you aren't capable of behaving like an adult, of being independent—and they think that if they tell you to shove it up your ass, you will get worse.

It is interesting to note that Giuseppe labels his own behavior as pathological and undifferentiated from the other family members. The therapist redirects attention to the subsystemic differentiation.

The therapist does not attack the parents directly. He points out how their love and concern for Giuseppe lead them to protect yet stigmatize him.

In this first session the therapist has *upset and disturbed the expectations of the family for reconsolidating the stability of the system.* By strategically negating the pathology and the involuntary aspects of Giuseppe's behavior, while accepting his central role, the therapist has blocked the attempt to reinstate the old rules of the relationship (Haley, 1963). In offering himself as the emotional point of reference for all the members of the system, the therapist communicates his unwillingness to become involved in their relational game. While challenging their dysfunctional organization by provoking the patient, he refuses to accept any response which repeats the old family script. He creates an action leading to *differentiation among the individual family members in respect to himself*, preventing any communication which he does not mediate.

Defining the patient's behavior as logical, voluntary, and useful shakes the stability of the system. Other family members will be stressed to show how the identified patient cannot possibly behave in logical, voluntary ways, much less in ways useful to the family.

The following excerpts from the subsequent session illustrate how the family counterreacts in relation to the interventions in the previous session (Haley, 1971):

Mother: You probably don't know about it, but after we were here last Tuesday, Giuseppe was worse than ever on Wednesday, Thursday, and Friday. He was in a terrible state, locked up in his room all day . . .

As predicted, the family claims that the situation became worse as a result of the previous session. Their message is clear: "Therapy is useless, even dangerous . . . but . . . help us anyway."

Father: In complete isolation . . . now what do you think we should . . .

Mother: He was just lying there on his bed almost the whole time. We were worried. . . . We talked to Doctor X about putting Giuseppe in the hospital for a while . . .

Giuseppe: I brought my law books to the hospital with me so I could study a little, because at the end of October I have to get sworn in as a practicing attorney. . . . I guess I was still thinking about continuing work with my brother, who's a lawyer.

Giuseppe's message and behavior continue to communicate the contradictory aspects of the same reality: the need for differentiation and the need for cohesion. Simultaneously, an autonomous aspect of Giuseppe's behavior comes to the fore: his concern about exams and his future career as a lawyer. Giuseppe implicitly calls attention to the absurdity of his hospitalization, which he "planned to utilize as a normal study period."

Therapist: I don't understand who it is that thinks you are better off in the hospital in these circumstances.

Giuseppe: Are you asking me?

Therapist: Yes, because I have a feeling that you want me to think that your family wants to get rid of you. But it really looks as though it's your system for gaining a sort of Pyrrhic victory over them.

The therapist continues to focus directly on the identified patient.

Giuseppe: In what way?

Therapist: By creating a big fuss, by going into the hospital to create a fuss. That's clear, isn't it?

The therapist affirms that Giuseppe's hospitalization was voluntary. It was Giuseppe himself who decided to go to the hospital, not because he was sick but to attract attention.

Giuseppe: By creating a fuss in what sense?

Therapist: In the sense that your parents would have to visit you, worry about all sorts of things, stay with you all the time . . .

The therapist begins to differentiate and define the spaces and functions of the other family members through the behavior of the identified patient.

Giuseppe: But they seem to be just as worried when I'm home, since lots of times . . .

Therapist: Don't shift the problem to your parents.

The therapist persists in his efforts to deprive the patient of control over family relations and to prevent the other family members from intruding into Giuseppe's personal space.

Giuseppe: My mother told me several times that the situation is intolerable.

Therapist: Let's not talk about your mother—you are the one who chose to go to the hospital.

The therapist reemphasizes the voluntary aspects of Giuseppe's behavior.

Giuseppe: It's not true that I chose to go, I really didn't want to go there . . . but my brother and

my cousin bugged me so much
that I just had to go.

Therapist: You know, I can accept
the fact that you don't want to
cooperate—but last time you
were more frank.

Giuseppe: What do you mean about
accepting that I don't want to cooperate?

Therapist: What I mean is that you   The therapist explicitly affirms that
are playing the part of the guy   every member of the family has a
who needs a crutch, and you   specific role and function and that
force your parents to try to con-   these are reciprocally complemen-
vince you to be a good boy . . .   tary. This is the reason that any
and then you even try to insinu-   change would be dangerous, unless
ate that they should feel guilty   it serves to reinforce the system's
about the way you behave. Right   homeostasis. The therapist's posi-
now you (*to the parents*) seem to   tion amounts to strategically deny-
be very upset by Giuseppe's ef-   ing therapy, or, "I am doing ther-
forts to blackmail you—he tries   apy, to avoid doing therapy."
to kill himself if you can't pay
enough attention to him. So we
can't begin family therapy unless
this situation remains exactly the
way it is. You will have to avoid
changing anything, because you
have all learned how to live with
this situation, and you all accept
it.

THE THERAPIST AS HOMEOSTATIC REGULATOR

The therapist introduces an unpredictable quality to the "input" of
the therapy, while reinforcing the homeostatic component. The unpredictability is directed not only at the logic of the family itself but also at the "socially accepted" logic of what constitutes a psychothera-
peutic intervention. Pursuing this line, he asks Giuseppe to have his
brothers and sister come to the following session, claiming that because his condition is reportedly worsening, his brothers must be pres-

ent to help and support his parents. By broadening the system in this way, the therapist redefines the problem in terms of parental authority over their children. He also changes the focus on the patient's symbolic behavior. A redistribution of the tensions and conflicts in the personal space and interactions of each one begins to be delineated.

In the following session Giuseppe, his parents, his two brothers and his sister are present. Franco is 36 years old and practices law in the northern city where he lives. Vito is 34, married, and works in a bank in a different town. Giovanna is 22, attends a university and comes home every weekend.

Franco: We think it might help if he left home . . . I don't know . . . now that we have this commitment to family therapy underway.

Therapist: The therapy truthfully isn't underway. It's barely started . . . here we begin to work only with families which have certain presuppositions.

The therapist strategically denies the therapy. He thereby forces the members of the system to research, individuate, and try out new relational and personal patterns using him, for now, as the point of reference.

Franco: Presuppositions? . . .

Therapist: Yes, presuppositions! In your case I don't feel we can start family therapy; above all because it seems to me . . . it seems to me that your parents feel like they're being blackmailed and they feel extremely troubled.

Franco: But I think . . . I have the feeling that maybe it was the family that damaged him . . . with a certain kind of upbringing . . . a certain attitude . . . perhaps not right for today's world.

Therapist: Ah, well wait . . . one
moment . . . this is a different
story . . . you think that it is the
family who makes trouble for
Giuseppe and not Giuseppe who
makes trouble for the family.

Franco: Well, let's say that right
now Giuseppe is giving trouble
to the family, but in the past . . .

Father: Well it's worth a try, but
until he's regained some sort of
balance . . . I don't know . . .
what you do say?

Mother: Yes . . . Doctor, what
would you advise us to do?

Therapist: I can't understand what
help you can possibly get from
these family sessions. . . . I can't
see any advantage to you in it
because this is a family which
cannot possibly change certain
attitudes in certain spheres, not
through anybody's fault.

Franco: Now you've got to help me
understand where we're lacking
. . . in what way are we not able
to . . .

The therapist takes this view of the
problem and clarifies its differentiating value.

Father and Mother keep trying to
bring the therapist into the center
of the discussion.

By denying the usefulness of therapy, the therapist introduces an unpredictable and destabilizing element. The family has no choice but
to continue in its attempt at transformation.

At this point the therapist dramatizes the family's situation: They
must all hold hands to graphically represent "how well this family functions when they are all united." Each one is asked to stay "together"
with the others but to distance himself at the same time. When asked to
break the circle, the subsystems of the couple and the children separate. At the end of this sequence they return to their previous positions,
with the identified patient between his parents again. Nevertheless,
each one has assumed a different position in the family and through
this metaphoric differentiation the possibilities for change have been
tested.

The therapist continues along this line:

Therapist (*to the mother*): Did you feel better before or now?

Mother: Without Giuseppe, Doctor, . . . well, at this point I would really feel better without Giuseppe . . . with my husband and my daughter, if she'd like to stay . . .

Therapist: How do you think your husband feels about it?

Mother: Well, uh, in this situation . . . maybe not as good as I do. . . . He doesn't really want Giuseppe out of the house.

Father: No, no, you see with three attempts at suicide. . . . We have to see that he regains some balance . . . some small . . .

Therapist: Okay. Let's hear what his brothers have to say.

The therapist works here through the differentiation within the subsystem.

Franco: It's all right with me. . . .

Therapist: Do you think Giuseppe will give you the same trouble he gives your parents?

Franco: No, absolutely not.

Therapist: This is a great affirmation you're making . . . it's mighty risky. . . . I don't believe the family causes Giuseppe's strange behavior . . . but from what you're saying, one could conclude that if Giuseppe breaks away he'll behave in a completely different way . . .

Giuseppe: But, look here . . . my situation is a terrible mess.

The identified patient takes the center again, speaking about the con-

. . . I just can't seem to do anything . . .

Franco: The only way he's going to
regain his balance is if we agree
about some mistakes which were
made . . . let me say it . . . because I didn't raise him or edu-
cate him . . . certain restrictions
. . . religion.

Giuseppe: Excuse me, no . . .no
. . . let's not begin now . . . because when I've had those break-
downs . . .

Franco: Let me finish! Then you
can deny it but later please. The
fact is, they, Momma and Papa,
consider us black sheep . . . because we live our own lives,
while you were the good one
. . . and since you were the good
one you felt supported in every
way, but then, at a certain point,
you became paralyzed.

Father: Is that true Giuseppe? What
do you say?

Giuseppe: But no . . . no . . .   .

Franco: Now I'll ask a question. Is
it true or not true that you considered him your golden boy and
that we were some sort of devi-
ants, or do you want to deny
that too?

Therapist: I feel it will be very risky
to try family therapy . . . I feel
there are many dangers . . . because you are a family with a lot
of energy and many differences
among you . . . and if we start

flicting situation which looms over
him (Haley, 1963).

The tension has mounted. The conflict between the parents' and the
children's subsystems has sharpened
and the identified patient is trying
to save the day.
Franco doesn't let Giuseppe intervene. Avoiding the family's usual
falsely protective attitude toward
Giuseppe, he treats him "normally."

The therapist seems to inhibit the
process of differentiation as being
dangerous to the family equilibrium. After having brought out the
differences, he underscores the risk
of differentiation. Strategically

therapy these differences will surface . . . it would be very risky.

negating the therapy, he moves them to a homeostatic pole and pushes the family to an imbalanced position.

Attempting to put an end to the confrontation between parents and children, Giuseppe quickly intervenes and again goes over his problem of sodomy with a woman and his fear of dying and burning in hell. But from the moment that the therapist takes over the position of stabilizing the homeostasis, the contradictions condensed into Giuseppe's symptomatic behavior become the content (sexuality, morality, religion) of a generational conflict, as well as a conflict between the parents. With the therapist acting as the stabilizing element, the function of the patient becomes less essential and the moments in which he is triangulated occur less frequently.

Therapist: Again I feel that, even though we have more information, we're still a long way from being able to start therapy. . . . Above all, I fear for you (*indicating Giuseppe*) because I don't want you to do anything hasty, to change the way you are . . . this would be dangerous. Your father and mother could suddenly find themselves facing an abyss. . . . Your father could have a heart attack or your mother could go into a depression. . . . Franco could feel that he was sucked in again and he might begin to be careless in his work. . . . Giovanna might lose her thoughtfulness, discover that she just can't meet her obligations. She might break up with her boyfriend and feel she has to

It is evident that the therapist, while strategically remaining at the homeostatic pole, has started individuating the areas of conflict and lack of satisfaction linked to each one's function in this rigid relational game. The anticipation of catastrophic change is introduced in a reassuring context where the therapist guarantees the maintaining of homeostasis.

return to the house to help your
mother. . . . Vito could develop
anxiety, feeling guilty about not
doing enough. . . .

Following through on his earlier position, the therapist again states
his doubts about the advisability of going on with therapy. He prescribes that Giuseppe "remain watchful and maintain his function as a
guarantee to the therapist."

In the next session he congratulates Giuseppe because he managed
to maintain his function with exceptional coherence.

Therapist: Before we begin I want
to compliment Giuseppe for ful-
filling my prescription so well.
Let's see how everyone else can
help him in this . . .
Franco: Listen, Doctor . . . I was
thinking of helping him get a job
. . . since it's about time for
some openings I had him make
out an application . . .
Therapist: But don't you know
your brother is commited to his
work at this moment?
Franco: Yes, he's involved in this
therapy here . . .
Therapist: No, that's not what I
mean. . . . Giuseppe is committed to his job in the family which
no one else can fill. You saw it
clearly. Didn't he seem to you to
be a person who was terribly oc-
cupied?

The guarantee consists in keeping things as they are. Keeping this
a fixed point, the therapist, in session, raises the spectre of what might
happen if Giuseppe were to give up his function. In this way he intro-

duces the "spectre of change," symbolized by the death of the patient. He tests the fears and the fantasies existent in the two subsystems, parental and filial.

Therapist (*to the parents*): Which of the two of you would be more devastated by Giuseppe's death?

Mother: I would be tortured by remorse all of my life.

Father: The pain would be immeasurable . . . but I wouldn't feel any guilt.

Therapist: You, Mrs. Fraioli, were you saying that Giuseppe would continue to maintain his function?

Mother: You know, Doctor, about . . . about the sexual problems . . . maybe I should have spoken with my husband . . . but instead I only cry . . . I resolve everything with tears . . .

Therapist: You mean Giuseppe's sexual problems?

Father: Yes, ours finished some time ago.

Mother: Naturally ours finished . . . also because Giuseppe's problems had an effect on our physical rapport . . .

Father: Yes, we became frigid.

Mother: Just to have heard Giuseppe mention that kind of sex . . . to think of the possibility that he eavesdropped . . .

Father: It ended up that all desire was killed . . .

Therapist: If I understand correctly, you're saying that Giuseppe took on all the sexuality of the family?

Turning to the siblings, the therapist explores each one's fantasies and exposes the function of the identified patient in relation to their breaking away.

Franco: I understand the roots of the situation . . . he was always with our parents, closer and closer . . . the model child . . . he was the preferred one . . .

Giovanna: Well, yes, because of him we were allowed to be pretty free . . . he was sort of the center and we others were more able to do what we wanted because he was there.

Therapist: Who among the six of you would feel it the most if the situation were to change?

Franco: Perhaps my parents.

Giovanna: At least Papa has a profession which involves him . . . I think it would be Mama . . .

Giuseppe: But you . . . how do you account for my prickish actions?

The identified patient again calls attention to himself as the central element, the patient.

Therapist: Even though Giuseppe continues to help me by guaranteeing his behavior, I need more. I would like all of you, together with your father and mother, to meet and look in depth at who might have the worst of it if you continue to come here. I want you to think about the energy and the help that you would eventually have to offer this person . . . because I don't believe that a therapy which provokes someone's collapse is acceptable.

Certain steps toward Giuseppe's autonomy are made possible by the therapist's having assumed the function of guaranteeing the homeostasis of the family and through the redistribution of tensions in both personal space and interactive space between the subsystems. In the succeeding months, while his siblings continue their involvement and the confrontation between the generations deepens (Minuchin, 1974), Giuseppe does begin to leave the house and gets interested in his studies. The problem of the "reciprocal breaking away" of the parents and the children becomes more and more apparent. Yet, the therapist knows that the family cannot acknowledge this improvement because that would require a change of rules which, though dysfunctional at one level, protect the integrity of the family at another level. For this reason, shortly after starting the next session, centered anew on the triad of mother-father-identified patient, the therapist takes the initiative by disqualifying the obvious improvement. He uses humor to accomplish this: On one hand he denies the improvement, but on the other he engages them as partners in this complicity.

Therapist (*a few minutes after the beginning of the session*): Giuseppe, I'd like to ask you right away whether you've had any new problems this week, because I can see from your face you are . . . less on guard than usual.

The therapist immediately disqualifies the obvious improvement.

Giuseppe: What do you mean?
Therapist: You are less on guard. What has happened?
Giuseppe: I'm a little confused.
Therapist: I'm not interested in the usual things. I want to know if there's been some big problem, something exceptional.

The therapist envisages a situation that is worse than the family's most dire fantasies. Therefore, whatever the family members say about the deterioration of the situation will fall short of the therapist's expectations.

Giuseppe (*surprised*): No, no really big problems.

Therapist: I must be mistaken then, but . . .

Father: We had an enormous problem in bringing him here, because this morning . . .

Therapist: But that's just a normal problem. . . . Giuseppe, I definitely have the feeling that you are less on guard.

Giuseppe: What do you mean? I don't know what you mean.

Mother: Forgive me for butting in, but maybe the doctor is talking about the fact that you did some extra activities . . .

The mother gives the therapist important feedback as to an understanding of the logic of functions. In this way the process of association is inverted. In the beginning it was the therapist who associated himself to the family; now it is vice versa and they are using the therapist's logic and punctuation.

Therapist: Mrs. Fraioli, you must have a sixth sense.

Mother: I think you (*to Giuseppe*) should tell the doctor that you worked at your desk two or three times.

Therapist: Ah, that's the reason you seem less on guard.

The therapist continues to define Giuseppe's improvement negatively.

Father: Even though he said that everything is useless, that it doesn't do any good. You said that right afterwards, didn't you? You said you would do something self-destructive.

Giuseppe: I know perfectly well that if some day I decide to do the same things my brothers do, I'll manage perfectly well, but I would have to give up . . .

Therapist: Your function.

Giuseppe: I don't know what . . .
I'd have to give up a fantasy
world.

Therapist: Your function, and I   The provocative aspect of this mes-
think you're being very naive by   sage is evident to the patient and to
behaving differently—naive be-   the entire system.
cause you are under the illusion
that someone else can or wants
to take over your function, that
perhaps someone else could do it
better than you. Can you suggest
someone?

Giuseppe: What did you say? I
didn't hear you.

Therapist: Can you suggest someone else . . . someone who can
take over your position at home,
who would be as watchful as
you are?

The therapist persists in defining Giuseppe's new attitude as inop-
portune and dangerous for the family's stability. He terminates the session by assigning a task intended to reinforce the system's dysfunctional rules (Andolfi & Menghi, 1977).

* The parents are instructed to observe closely all abnormal behavior on Giuseppe's part. They are to discuss his behavior
  each evening, recording all details in a notebook.
* Giuseppe is told to stay home for the following two weeks. He
  is not to modify his usual behavior in any way. Any adult behavior on his part, whether voluntary or prompted by his parents, will be considered a breach of the agreement and a failure
  to uphold his vital function in the family.
* Giuseppe and his parents are asked to guarantee that the instruction will be scrupulously carried out. They are asked to
  note any *transgressions* in writing.
* The following session will be held only if the participants submit the written material requested.

The therapist reconfirms his support of the family's homeostatic tendencies by defining any future autonomous moves by Giuseppe as a betrayal of his family function. He actually instructs Giuseppe to persist in his symptomatic behavior and requests the family to observe certain family rules faithfully. The rules that the therapist specifically prescribes are those concerning Giuseppe and his parents' close surveillance of each other's behavior. In carrying out these instructions the family will be forced to take cognizance of its real situation, which will rapidly appear intolerable to each of the members. The ultimate objective of this strategy is to strengthen generational boundaries and to permit greater individual autonomy.

Giuseppe and his parents bring a series of written notes to the following session. These notes are utilized by the family to contradict the therapist's view concerning the importance of Giuseppe's function. Moreover, the notes indicate that Giuseppe went out of the house on several occasions to visit a friend and that he was irritated by his parent's continual anxiety.

The following is part of the recorded notes brought to the next session by Giuseppe, his father and his mother. The material follows a natural time sequence.

Father

The contrast between Giuseppe's negative position, which you consider "coherent," and his attempt to construct an autonomous existence appears most clear.

As far as the recurrent idea of suicide is concerned, it seems more and more to be a sort of blackmail. Sometimes when I talk to him about it he admits that his behavior is planned to make us commiserate with him.

Total Isolation. He was able to study in the evening. When he starts on his destructive speeches I always react by trying to talk him out of it. I'm always ready to try—it's almost an instinctive reaction.

This morning he went to the courthouse with his brother. When he got home he said he was wasting his time. He stayed in bed in the afternoon and then went out without any special plan in mind. He came in at about 9:30 and at supper he spoke affectionately about Vito's children. Then all of a sudden his mood darkened again and there was nothing I could do to reach him.

In the morning he went to the courthouse again. He studied after lunch and then went to the athletic field. He studied again when he got home and after dinner he went out again until midnight. He seemed in a normal, good mood but about 1 a.m. he awoke asking for a sleeping pill. He couldn't fall asleep and he seemed upset about something.

My wife went to visit our granddaughter and I stayed home with Giuseppe. I was prepared to have a hard time but, surprisingly, Giuseppe was relaxed and even cooperative. He studied in his own room and I didn't go in to check on him at all . . . and nothing happened. I believe now that our nagging drove him to do things that worried us but also gave us a "kick."

Mother

This morning he went to the athletic field for about an hour wearing his running suit. When he came home he started to study. In the afternoon he went out for an hour and he looked upset when he came home. When I asked him if something special happened, he told me he was always haunted by the idea of injuring himself. He got into bed and his father pleaded with him to get up and read a bit in one of his legal books (incorrect on the part of his father).

He's not paying real attention to his work with his brother. In the afternoon he made a lame attempt to study but didn't accomplish anything. He had a dour expression. Then he went out. He was away for two hours and I was very worried. When he got home he didn't want any dinner but then later he took something to eat alone.

In the morning he stayed in bed until noon and seemed very depressed (as usual). Then he left to see his friend Federico. Giuseppe had really wanted to see him and they spoke for an hour and a half, strangely enough. After lunch he went out again to look for one of his old high school friends. He came home again around 3 o'clock and then went out again. An hour later he came in, took a shower, changed his clothes and studied from about 4 until 7.

Giuseppe's state of mind seems changed. He doesn't seem depressed. In fact, he seems almost euphoric. After dinner he called two acquaintances and later he accepted an invitation from Franco to meet with some other lawyers in the morning to file some legal forms.

This morning I had barely been able to rouse him and pleaded with him to react to his depression.

After he met Franco and submitted his legal papers he went to see a friend. In the afternoon he went to bed and woke up at 6 in a nasty mood. He kept repeating that he must resign himself to living in the old way. He said he wanted to steal some pornographic magazines. Then he went out and called a little later to tell me that he was having dinner at a friend's house.

For the most part, today, Giuseppe didn't fulfill his function. In the morning he went to the courthouse and took an oral exam which might put him in the position to take an examination for a prosecutor's position. He stayed home for a while in the afternoon and I tried to encourage him, help him react, to give him some confidence. He went out at about 7. He had an appointment to go to the movies after dinner but he didn't go. He was weeping, saying that when I won't be around he won't have anyone in the world in whom he can confide.

Giuseppe

You can't escape reality. So, if I go along with the pretense of family therapy, or if I don't, there's still no escape. The others don't do anything they're not supposed to do in relation to me.

In this period I've done what I could. Wednesday morning I went to see my friend Matteo. I had called him to see if he'd help me fix up the boat. Then I went to Franco's office. But it's all really useless. You can't escape reality. Sure I can go to Franco's, but that doesn't change anything . . . it just might be better to end it all now instead of going on with this farce.

I kept going to Franco's office; I went to dinner with a friend, an old high school friend. Maybe the only thing I can do now is to passively accept this situation, make up my mind to continue to go to Rome even if this therapy won't change anything. But passive resistance in an absurd situation is impossible!

At the end of the session the therapist states his displeasure at the poor cooperation with his therapeutic prescription and at the lightness with which Giuseppe is taking his diminished function within the family.

CHANGE AS A CHALLENGE TO THE THERAPIST

A new phase begins here which is characterized by the progressive *decentralization of the therapist.* This will culminate in the separation of the therapeutic system. Decentralization will continue until the interactive space of the new structure of the system can be verified and tested (Menghi, 1977).

In this first phase the therapist is still responsible for maintaining the system's homeostasis, replacing the centralized function of the identified patient. Greater individuation in personal space and subsystem space begins to appear. The family insists that improvement is occurring in response to the therapist's earlier challenge contained in the strategic denial of the improvement.

While deepening and extending the personal and subsystemic space, the therapist remains in the position of one who denies the usefulness of change, warning of the difficulties and the risks involved. At this point, the risks are no longer intrinsic but are tied to the concrete demands which each one is beginning to look for in his relationship with the others. The intervention, therefore, must now hold no threat to the homeostasis of the family. If anything, it must represent an obstacle to the first rumblings of change. It is through the removal of these posed obstacles, designed to show the therapist how unfounded his fears are, that the family arrives at greater autonomy.

The following excerpts are from the 13th session, in which only the parents participated.

Mother: Now I'm feeling tired, beat.
    I think I'll take a little rest . . .
Father: But I can sum things up. It's   In this phase, the father participates
true, Giuseppe has changed recent-   more actively and responsibly.
    ly . . . he hasn't stayed in bed at
    all. He went to court a few times

with his brother, he has done
some studying . . . he is always
carrying his books around . . .
Therapist: Children's books?

The therapist interrupts, expressing
incredulity. His tone is provocative,
but also light and humorous.

Father: No, law books. He really
has made an effort to straighten
out. True, if I ask him about it,
he says, "I'm doing this but I'm
convinced it's all over for me."
But he used to be consistent in
this completely negative attitude
. . . he stayed at home. Now, if
his brother calls him down to the
courthouse, he goes.

Therapist: I'm not convinced by all
of this. I'm surprised that after
all of the experiences you've had,
you believe in it so blindly.

. . . but the therapist is also saying
"even though you've had such negative experiences I would like to believe that you still hope for something positive."

Father: It's not that I believe in it
. . . I'm wondering, I'm telling
you about it . . .

Therapist: I'm trying to tell you
that I don't believe in it. I didn't
expect to find any improvements
today. At the most a few well-re-
hearsed scenes . . . but nothing
that would be so dangerous for
all of you.

The therapist emphasizes that they
must take on the risks inherent in
change.

Mother: In my opinion, Giuseppe
is making progress.

Now both parents agree that an
improvement has taken place. It
seems as though the therapist's
doubts have reinforced the parents'
conviction.

Father: But don't you understand
that just a minute ago the doctor
said that he doesn't believe in
Giuseppe's efforts to rehabilitate

himself? He said it in so many
words: "I don't believe in it,"
and maybe he has good reasons.
It's true that Giuseppe says, "I
should look for a job," and then
he says, "But I can't."

Mother: At this point I want to say
something. From the 15th to the
26th—I've got it written down
right here—those were all good
days. Giuseppe spent all of those
mornings at his brother's office,
and he stayed home very little.

Father: We shouldn't be convinced,
I agree. The boy might do something crazy tomorrow, but in
fact . . . another positive thing
has happened. Giuseppe won a
case and we only found out
about it from the newspaper. We
didn't even know he was working on this case, so I think, that
is, we're careful not to get our
hopes up too high—even Franco,
who is always cautious and never
goes overboard in his judgments,
said to my wife yesterday . . .

Mother: He has noticed that Giuseppe seems more interested in
his work.

Father: Yes, he says that Giuseppe
has some real interest in his
work.

Therapist: I still don't trust all of
this—it's too risky. Giuseppe
can't just give up his function
like this. You haven't given me
sufficient guarantees.

The parents want to convince the
therapist that an improvement has
occurred. If the therapist accepts
this view, the family's collective efforts toward improvement would
probably come to a halt. The therapist does not budge from his position of incredulity. This position is
paradoxically reassuring to the
family and allows the system to
move further in the direction of
change.

The therapist implies that his doubts
can be allayed only if more substan-
tial changes can be demonstrated.

Even though the therapist has introduced the idea of further change,
he spends the rest of the session warning the family not to modify their

habitual modalities of interaction. In particular, the therapist insists that Giuseppe should continue to play the role of watchman—a role that is extremely useful to everyone and that he plays with perfect self-abnegation.

The repetition of the behavior prescribed by the therapist imprisons each one within the limited space of his function and creates increasing irritation. The parents begin to feel the weight of their control over Giuseppe. The more that their control surfaces and the more it is prescribed by the therapist, the more it is perceived with a "sense of the ridiculous," as evidenced in this account of the mother's:

> At 5:30 Giuseppe went out to go to evening mass, saying he would come right back. By 7:30 he hadn't returned yet and I was very upset—worried about this. So after calling his friend Matteo to see if he was there, my husband went to the train station that Giuseppe always talked about. Right after his father left, Giuseppe came home, saying he had gone to see a friend. When he heard that his father had gone out looking for him, he scowled and became silent. Later, after his father, who was a bit embarrassed, returned, he was able to talk to us, scolding us for our apprehension. Thinking it over now, the whole thing seems out of proportion . . . even a bit ridiculous . . . if it weren't for his earlier behavior. . . . Even now while I'm writing I ask myself how long am I going to continue writing how many times Giuseppe does this or that . . . besides, he's getting more and more "rebellious" and "defiant."

Giuseppe, for his part, acts more and more rebellious. He sends messages about how intolerable the family "style" is:

> If we can ever reach a point where each one will stay in his own sphere without feeling everybody's eyes on him. . . . It seems impossible that we'll ever get there! As for me, they're always breaking my balls, "This, yes." "This, no . . . "

All of this creates increased tension, which the system expresses through Giuseppe in the 14th session. An explosion occurs and Giuseppe refuses to participate in subsequent sessions.

Giuseppe: This idea of going to a psychiatrist and talking about your own fucking business is completely ambivalent. NO! You can all go and shove it up your ass. I accept my life just as it is, so stop bugging me. Goddamn it all, I don't bug you, so lay off me. Then we'll be even!

Therapist: I think Giuseppe is telling us in his way that he doesn't feel like whining today. I'm very pleased. I wasn't expecting it.

The therapist defines Giuseppe's statements as positive, showing his attempt to impose limits between himself and the others. "I wasn't expecting it" means "I wasn't expecting that he would express so openly his suffering in having to always show the most monotonous and squalid part of himself."

A NEW STRUCTURE

The therapeutic team interprets Giuseppe's absence from the subsequent sessions as a positive development. It confirms that an important structural change has occurred. Previously, the family system could not tolerate any distance between Giuseppe and his parents, and particularly between mother and son; therefore, the parents' decision to continue therapy without Giuseppe is indicative of an important structural modification. The parents are able to come alone without feeling paralyzed by the anxiety which bound them to their son. They even manage to go out together one evening, leaving Giuseppe home alone. Mother recounts the episode in his way:

My husband and I went out after dinner leaving Giuseppe home. He wasn't completely relaxed and held a jumprope in his hand. We came home at midnight and he was already in bed. The light was on so we went in to say good night. When we told him we'd gone to the movies he said it must have been a mighty long time since we had last done that.

According to the parents' reports, Giuseppe has also become more autonomous. Several sessions are devoted to consolidating the newly established distance between parents. The therapist then sends a letter to Giuseppe via his parents.

The therapist's letter to the identified patient is intended:

1) To acknowledge Giuseppe's efforts to consolidate a more autonomous position.
2) To renew the strategy of provocation by again prescribing the patient's symptomatology.
3) To further a sharper delineation of boundaries between the parent subsystem and the patient.
4) To establish an equivalence between Giuseppe's autonomy and that of the parents.

The text of the letter is as follows:

Dear Giuseppe:
I realize that you have been making a considerable effort to participate more effectively in family therapy. Your participation from a distance is particularly constructive for you, because there is no risk of your becoming dependent or passive toward therapy. I hope that you will continue to behave as creatively as you have in the past (stay in bed as much as possible, masturbate frequently, bug the rest of the family, threaten to commit self-destructive acts, don't work, etc.), until you are absolutely certain that your parents will be able to carry on alone and that they no longer need your function.

The therapist gives the letter to the parents with the following instructions:

* The letter should be read aloud daily by either the father or the mother in the presence of the other spouse and Giuseppe.
* After each reading, all three should discuss their thoughts about it.
* If Giuseppe refuses to participate, the letter should be read by the parents at the set hour in another place or outside of the house.

    * The following session will be held only if these instructions
    have been carried out.

The letter reinforces the general strategy utilized in this phase, redefines Giuseppe's behavior as creative, and focuses attention on the
functional characteristics of the family system. It is similar in form to
the messages of the identified patient who, when he does something
positive, needs to define it as negative, and, when he acts autonomously, needs to quickly compensate with some symptomatic behavior.

Although the letter is formally addressed to Giuseppe, it is really addressed to the entire family system. In fact, the entire family reacts to it.
The third instruction (the parents should read the letter outside of the
house if Giuseppe is absent) provides another opportunity for the parents to confront each other and strengthen their conjugal relationship
while separating themselves from their son.

Giuseppe's increasing movement toward greater autonomy requires
parallel movement in the structure of the parents' subsystem.

In subsequent sessions with the parents, the therapist, stressing the
impossibility of the couple's exchanges without triangulating with Giuseppe (reinforced by the reading of the letter at home), helps them bring
to the surface their own needs for personal as well as shared space
which no longer revolves around discussing Giuseppe's pathology.

Now the therapist is ready to use a more typical structural approach.
He will *test for the strength of a new structure by giving up his function
as their homeostatic regulator* and assess the family's capacity for reorganization without needing the presence of pathology as its fulcrum. In
this phase the structural intervention is involved with supervising the
alternative interactions autonomously performed by the family in its
search for a new dynamic equilibrium (Andolfi, 1979).

In one of the mother's accounts reported after the reading of the letter it appears that the parents have reached a more objective understanding of the situation. She says:

    . . . one might think that we've been the gainers of Giuseppe's
    function so that we can carry on alone. But it seems to me that we
    aided and abetted him and have also been conditioned by him.
    This conditioning would end if he were to assume logical, adult

attitudes. In any case, I, as his mother, know full well that we must force ourselves not to be conditioned by his function. On the other side of it, I seem to see a tentative move on his part to get back into the larger world. For example, when we returned from our night out in Rome we noticed that he had planned and prepared his own supper. This makes me think that he can acquire more autonomy and independence if we can let go.

Here it seems that the parents have made a courageous decision to work with the help of the therapist against their own need of Giuseppe's function.

The following excerpts are from two sessions where only the parents were present. This is significant in that it shows the passage from triangulation of the couple with Giuseppe to greater differentiation within the couple. In the course of this process one may see that the position of the therapist is increasingly decentralized.

Mother: You know, I feel that in the end Giuseppe will finish . . . finish somewhat by following my path.
Therapist: In what sense?
Mother: In his social relations . . . I think he has the same timidity, afraid of having much to do with others that I had . . .
Father: But with me you were outgoing . . . you were only closed to others but, to tell you the truth, I liked it that way . . . maybe it's my character . . . all this going out, moving here and there . . . I wouldn't have much liked it.
Mother: It was fine for me too but at a certain point I realized it wasn't good for our children . . . and maybe it wasn't good for me either . . . many times I reproved myself for not having made friends . . . for being too closed . . .
Father: But when you found a person who suited you, you opened up . . .
Therapist: That was you?
Father: That was me.
Mother: But we haven't done . . . yes, we've cared for each other, we've had this family . . . but for ourselves we haven't accomplished much . . .

Father: Well, maybe now that the children are grown we can permit
ourselves some pleasure . . . it's true I've always been something
of a puritan.

At the end of the session, after husband and wife have reestablished
reciprocal interest through their reminiscences, the therapist makes a
request. He asks that, "while knowing that they are not ready for it,"
they telephone Giuseppe to tell him they are spending the night in Rome
and will return in the morning. He suggests that it isn't to do something positive for themselves but as a sort of "training," as an effort toward not being conditioned by their son's behavior (and their fears).
The couple absorbs this prescription with some perplexity (Andolfi &
Menghi, 1976). The father mentions business appointments, the mother, duties at home. They leave discussing whether or not it is possible.
The mother opens the next session by stating that they went to the
theater for the first time in many years.

Mother: I believe that we parents have to begin this process of letting
go of our children. . . . It will be a long, hard road . . . but I
really believe we can make it . . . for example I . . . maybe it's
ridiculous . . . but I joined the Alliance Français so I can begin
to study French again and go to lectures. I met some people I had
already known, like an old school chum who now teaches French
literature.
Father: And then . . . we decided to take a trip this summer for the
first time in years.
Therapist: I have the feeling that if you want to take this trip you have
to start building some credibility with your kids. (*He walks out.*)
Mother: Maybe he's right. Even Giovanna says, "I hope you really do
it." Perhaps we should start now with a weekend trip, go to the
country . . .
Therapist (*reentering*): My collaborators brought it to my attention
that this trip is still hypothetical. It's not at all a sure plan.
Father: Oh, I believe we're absolutely going to take that trip.
Therapist: But what would happen if somebody at home were to throw
out one of those "life-savers" . . . where someone who's afraid of
the water out there could grab onto . . . Giuseppe or even Giovanna could toss one out just to see what would happen.

Mother: What do you mean—what could one be?

Father: For example, Giuseppe could have one of his crises . . . but
   this time we wouldn't hang on!

Mother: No, no! It won't happen . . .

DISMANTLING THE THERAPEUTIC SYSTEM

In successive sessions husband and wife reaffirm their plan for taking this trip, outlining a detailed program. This occurs because each
one is involved with and committed to the other's real wish to have this
experience and it is not a function of the relationship with the therapist.
The accounts related to the reading of the letter by the parents have become a means to reflect upon their own past lives, their relationships
with their children, and their ties to their original families. They re-
mark with surprise and satisfaction that they have been able to spend
time speaking of Giuseppe while feeling free of guilt. They also emphasize that he appears improved in direct relation to their detachment.
They were overwhelmed by the fact that Giuseppe himself broke away
and took a trip to Assisi before they were to take theirs and they felt
"beaten at their own game."

Giuseppe gives continuous news of his own progress and defines his
behavior as "pretty much normal." His earlier symptomatology has
not reappeared, even though he states that he has not yet resolved his
problems. He defines these himself, in a letter sent to the therapist, as
"difficulty in making a decision, to know who he is and to enter the
adult world." This reflects a certain concern for the future, but he is
now actively engaged in his life process rather than pulled back into his
old regressive behavior. He passed a series of professional examina-
tions and is actively at work in his brother's law firm. He is also studying to keep his professional education up to date. He took a vacation
trip with some friends and was pleased by this new experience. He has
formed a close friendship with a young man of his own age and they
spend much free time together. He frequently visits his oldest brother,
who lives in a city nearby and has formed an important and meaningful
relationship with him. He is planning some trips for next year with
projects for visiting some interesting regions of Italy.

In a session following the vacation the parents state that they are full
of tensions related to their having "such different personalities" but re-

port that they also feel vitalized by these talks. The father says that he has "rediscovered" Giovanna, his daughter, and that his relationship with her, which had been interrupted without his realizing it, has been renewed. In a letter sent to the therapist after a year of therapy, the father again writes about this therapeutic experience:

> . . . Sincerely, I must say that our experience with you in these 23 sessions has been very successful and deeply involving but we've surely gained a renewed faith in ourselves and our ability to face what life holds, especially as we get older. . . . Giuseppe still isn't clear about professional choices open to him. . . . Giovanna is having her problems but I have a lot of faith in her intelligence and in the dialogue which has been reopened between us. . . . My wife and I hope that these signs of rebirth will continue. . . . I personally can guarantee my commitment. . . . I suddenly realize that I write to you as a friend and this seems to me to be a very positive point. . . . "

The gradual disengagement of the family from the therapeutic system renders the members more independent. Each one must now assume responsibility for the family's changed situation. In this sense each one, including the therapist, works on a balance sheet.

In this last phase of separation from the family, the therapist must be able to make that change pointed up so clearly by Mr. Fraioli, to *let go of the function of therapist,* in order to then meet the family members as a person with whom they may have a rapport, an exchange about matters no longer masked by pathology.

The following are excerpts from a conversation between Giuseppe and the therapist in the very final stages of therapy. It was Giuseppe himself who requested this meeting between the two of them alone in order to speak face to face.

Giuseppe: At this point I think it's time to be concrete, I mean to decide between "can't" or "won't." But it seems to me that the way life is, a person can't ever decide all by himself—you decide only a

part of it because there are always other factors that exist,
that make it easier or harder.
. . . In other words the problem
is this. . . . I have to say clearly
right now that in my relations
with the opposite sex I'm neither
here nor there, in the sense that
nowadays it's really difficult to
start a serious relationship with a
girl . . .

Therapist: I had a friend at school
who said that you had to go to a
hooker to do something. We always answered that it seemed
like such a squalid thing to do. It
finished up with us taking him to
one and he went through with it.
. . . Now it seems to me that
you are trying to deny something
at the same time that you do it.
. . . It's as if you would say,
"The real problem is with the
girls," but it isn't clear to me if
you "can't" or you "won't." Then
you say, "The fault is really with
the girls!" So it looks like you always look for some excuse for
not facing the problem. . . . It's
like the sodomy business . . . do
you remember?

The therapist can now speak openly about the contradictions inherent
in Giuseppe's messages.

Giuseppe: The first session, two
years ago.

Therapist: You remember too
about "shoving it up . . . "?
What was the difference between
you and me on that . . . ?

The context is intense. There is a
level of complicity which can exist
only between two people who have
shared a past history. The confrontation is direct, man to man.

Giuseppe: I don't remember exactly . . .

Therapist: You spoke of shoving it up an ass, but it seemed to me that the real idea was with a little word you used just before that . . .

Giuseppe: Supersodomy!

Therapist: Exactly—a special "shove it up" . . . my feeling is that you don't have trouble with women —we all do more or less, you know—the problem is that you expect I don't know what from a woman. Maybe then it was okay to masturbate with *Playboy* . . . but it's not really very satisfying . . .

Giuseppe: I would certainly say no.

Therapist: So the problem is in fact the lack of satisfaction you were talking about.

Giuseppe: Right . . . perpetual frustration.

Therapist: You know, in *Playboy* the women are pretty special. Did you ever see any who are even a little flabby?

Giuseppe: No.

Therapist: . . . or one who's beginning to show signs of aging?

Giuseppe: No, of course not.

Therapist: Well, those women are "super" beauties. And you prefer them to real women. You have a slight tendency to be extraordinary, to be "super."

Giuseppe: I must admit that what you're saying is true . . . that I want too much . . . but now I . . . I'd like . . . let me explain with a concrete example . . .

Giuseppe begins to talk about an encounter he had with a girl on a train, about his embarrassment, the discovery that they had interests in common, the pleasant surprise that she would be taking the same train back, and then his disappointment at not finding her when he looked for her in the same station.

Giuseppe: . . . Let's say . . . well, in theory, the opportunity may arise . . . but then it's difficult to find a practical approach . . . this was a special case because, even though I tried, I didn't find her again . . .

Therapist: In this case was it you "couldn't" or you "wouldn't"?

Giuseppe: No, in this case I really wanted to find her, I wanted it a lot . . . but it just didn't work out . . .

Therapist: You probably are still caught in this dilemma between "can" and "will," in the sense that there may still be some function you must fill . . . and therefore you can't allow yourself to do what you want . . . this dilemma is still present. You know up to a short time ago you couldn't have a relationship with a woman . . . probably you couldn't even have an adult relationship. . . . I mean talking with two grown-ups without whining. . . . Maybe you still might feel you have some function to fill . . . one that you hold dear . . . which is making it harder for you to feel that you are Giuseppe. When you first came here, you weren't Giuseppe;

The style is still provocative, but the therapist can openly give recognition to the changes which have taken place.

you were a mass of other things
. . . self-punishing, fixated . . .
blackmailing . . . do you recall?
There were innumerable functions you had to fill. I don't
know just where you are
now . . .

Giuseppe: I don't know . . . but
certainly things have changed
. . . and it's not easy to face the
problems around me . . . maybe
the others . . . I feel that I'm
without armor, defenseless . . .
above all with women . . .

Therapist: That's why I'm asking
why you should give up the functions at which you're such an expert . . . so that you become a
preadolescent or an adolescent
who's at his first conquest and
even blushes when he speaks
with a girl . . . and then I get the
feeling that you're still too interested in how you must respond
to others instead of thinking
about what you want to say.
What is it that you want for
yourself?

Giuseppe: I probably don't even
know what I really want . . .

Therapist: I'd like to get clear on
whether you want to do something for yourself or if you're still
committed to your functions . . .

Giuseppe: I don't really think so
. . . but I don't have an answer
right now . . . it's so difficult to
begin . . . but one thing is certain, now I can laugh at myself
more. . . . I take myself a lot less
seriously . . .

Even though the therapist maintains his provocative style to test Giuseppe's ability to know his own personal boundaries, his manner communicates that he is disposed to discussing the young man's difficulties at finding himself an awkward adolescent who must face his inadequacies. He is, however, now an adolescent who need no longer hide himself in a pathology. At this point perhaps Giuseppe may decide to try to meet his own needs through an individual therapy.*

The same holds true for the parents who, once they let go of their children, are able to face old as well as new problems without the need for pathologic triangulation. Now the therapist can finally openly recognize the change which has occurred and directly congratulate the family for both the massive efforts made and the results achieved. His dismantling of the rigidity present in this system, together with the concomitant opening toward new alternatives, is finished. *The ultimate evolution of the new structure lies with the family and its individual members* (Andolfi & Menghi, 1976).

CONCLUSIONS

We have attempted in the longitudinal reconstruction of the therapy of the Fraioli family to replicate through its process the approach presented in this book. One may delineate a part considered more "strategic," whose goal is to rupture the dysfunctional rigidity of the family system, and another part which may be defined as more "structural," whose goal is the organization of a new family structure (Stanton, 1981). In reality it is possible to see the unfolding of the same process: that of the *progressive differentiation of personal space* with consequent *loss of rigidity in the entire system* through the increase in its informative potential. The rupture of the rigidity of the system, which inhibits a satisfactory exchange, coincides with the activation of individual potential which was concealed by the reductive functions in the family drama. The freeing and the rediscovery of each one's personal

---

*In recent years we have encountered with some frequency a situation wherein, when a family therapy intervention is terminated successfully, a *request for individual therapy* is made either by the identified patient or another family member. We consider this evolution to be a positive result of the work done with the entire family system.

space give great impetus to creating new relational patterns within the system.

Through the use of *redefinition, provocation* and *strategic denial* (Andolfi, 1979; Andolfi et al., 1980), the therapist destabilizes the family system, affecting many levels.

* He accepts the centrality of the identified patient while completely subverting his raison d'être because he redefines the patient's behavior as logical, voluntary and useful.
* He further narrows the constricted personal space of the others, which coincides with the function assigned them in their specific family logic.
* He brings to the surface and separates the contradictions and conflicts within the symptomatic behavior, redistributing the tensions and stress in each one's personal as well as subsystemic space.
* He makes it difficult or even impossible to respond in old ways, with the old rules and old repetitious behaviors.
* He prevents the family from restabilizing a new equilibrium that is only a functional transformation identical with the previous one (Ashby, 1956).
* He brings fantasies and fears into the open, minimizing their destructive power.
* He activates face to face communication and helps draw together the individual needs and desires no longer hidden behind the pathology of one family member.

During this process the therapist initially takes the place of the identified patient, placing himself at the center and letting each one define himself or herself in terms of the therapist-as-central. In this way he uncovers the desires hidden behind each one's encounter with his own function. Since this is no longer applied in interactive space, the function loses its value as a shared behavior which has a goal and becomes merely an impoverished identity reduced to only one dimension. These same desires, which are often expressed as fantasies and always within the delimited structure where the therapist is the one responsible for maintaining the family homeostasis, in themselves represent new and destabilizing information.

Maintaining himself at the homeostatic pole and in the central position, the therapist *changes the facts of the interactive configuration of the system.* At the same time, he strategically denies the possibility of change. His object is to create a breach in the rigidity of the family system, to help family members relinquish their certainties and to begin to experiment with new personal and relational patterns. By continuously redefining, the therapist prevents the family from stabilizing itself around only one definition. He does not allow the family members to find a place for the therapeutic intervention in their old frame of reference. At the same time, new personal space is individuated and channels of interaction are reopened. These represent increased potential for communication and, therefore, greater possibility for restructuring.

Now it becomes possible to proceed toward the *verification of the new structure.* This is signaled by a movement from a strategic approach to one which is more typically structural. This passage is characterized by the progressive decentralization of the therapist until the point of arrival at the *dismantling of the therapeutic system.*

At an earlier stage, when the family claims it has effected changes as a function of the therapist and the challenges he has posed, he responds with the strategic denial of improvement having taken place. He shows a greater openness toward accepting the movement of the family system but he still requires its concrete verification. He seeks, therefore, a commitment which will show the visible results of these claims of change. The verification is initiated during the therapeutic session and carried over into the home. This reinforces the thrust toward change and extends the therapeutic process beyond the session. In doing this the therapist emphasizes the necessity for the family to take on the risks inherent in change. If the family is capable of finding new ways of communication for the therapist, it can also generalize the benefits of these changes among its own members. It can learn to function autonomously. At this stage, the therapist still retains the central role as the person responsible for maintaining homeostasis, indicating his doubts and questions relative to taking the risks involved in trying to change. This permits the family to move out of its old equilibrium toward change. This is seen in the increased ability of each one to seek individuation within the system.

A second phase begins here with the therapist's progressive removal of himself from the center and the family's verification of their experienced, changed relationship between personal space and interactive space. This does not connote the absence of problems and of conflicts, but demonstrates the capacity to face these problems without the need to masquerade behind a pathology. Confrontation within the family system is more direct, with the therapist functioning only as an activator. His interventions are now more typically structural. They are designed to help the members of the family define their individual and subsystemic boundaries and to put into practice new modes of relating within the system, as well as outside of it, creating future, practical solutions. The therapist may then function as a point of reference, someone to be seen periodically to examine the course of their new efforts.

The apparent simplicity of the therapeutic direction and the intelligibility of the interventions in this terminal phase seem so clear that it would be easy to underestimate their importance. However, superficiality or haste can cause the therapist to make serious errors. The therapist's moves at this time should lead to his own decentralization and to a gradual diminution of his power, which is no longer essential to the success of the therapy.

The *dismantling of the therapeutic system* ultimately results in the family's finding its own capacity for self-therapy, taking its new "input," internal and external, as an opportunity for growth and change. The final objective is that the process initiated be able to continue under its own direction without further need for therapeutic sessions.

Significantly, in the case of the Fraioli family the symptomatic behavior of the identified patient continues to undergo progressive redefinition. At the start, the therapist, firmly in the center, redefines the behavior as logical, voluntary, and useful. Later, after having extended and opened the father-mother-son triad to include the two brothers and the sister, he pragmatically redefines the problem as a generational conflict. By doing this he helps open the way for the passage from a vague, undifferentiated family emotional interplay centered around the symptom to a greater differentiation of the conflict. When the triad reconnects, the autonomy of the son is in relationship to the autonomy of the parents. This ultimate redefinition of the problem is reinforced by a clear division between the parental subsystem and the son's subsystem.

All of this change occurs in a context wherein the therapist remains responsible for maintaining the family homeostasis while prescribing the dysfunctional rules of the system in a provocative way and strategically denying each sign of improvement. The change which is fundamental to the therapeutic process occurs when the perception of the family is altered and family members no longer emphasize the pathology, but, rather, look at its relational significance. Only then can the search for autonomy begin to take hold. Fear of confrontation and fear of trying out the new patterns are the natural companions of this stage.

The first "feedback" of the newly gained conceptual and emotional image of their problems derived from the process of redefinition is that they can now face their problems rather than evade them (Watzlawick et al., 1974).

Their hopes and questions are now more personal. They need not be hidden behind symptomatology. The mother's diaries, initially centered on her son's pathological behavior, develop into personal documents reflecting upon her own life, examining the autonomy of the parental couple, its components and their relationship with their son.

In the course of the therapeutic process, the family becomes more and more a group of individuals, as opposed to a compact, reacting system. It becomes possible to create a new structure when the *relativity of the interpretation of reality* is again recognized. This comes about through the rediscovery of personal and subsystemic space and the realistic limitations which temper this new situation. The old choice of rigid functioning is no longer preferable to the threat of a loss of identity. This has become true for all of them, but particularly for the identified patient.

Bibliography

Alarcon, P. A. de. *L'amico della morte.* Milano: Ricci, 1978.

Andolfi, M. *Family therapy: An interactional approach.* Plenum Press: New York, 1979.

Andolfi, M., & Angelo, C. The therapist as director of the family drama. *Journal of Marital and Family Therapy,* 1981, 7, 3: 255–264.

Andolfi, M., & Menghi, P. La prescrizione in terapia familiare—Parte I. *Archivio di Psicologia, Neurologia e Psichiatria,* 1976, 4, 434–456.

Andolfi, M., & Menghi, P. La prescrizione in terapia familiare: Il paradosso therapeutico. *Archivio di Psicologia, Neurologia e Psichiatria,* 1977, 1, 57–76.

Andolfi, M., Menghi, P., Nicolò, A., & Saccu, C. Interaction in rigid systems: A model of intervention in families with a schizophrenic member. In M. Andolfi and I. Zwerling (Eds.), *Dimensions of family therapy.* New York: Guilford Press, 1980.

Angelo, C. The use of the metaphoric object in family therapy. *American Journal of Family Therapy,* 1981, 9, 1: 69–78.

Ashby, W. R. *An introduction to cybernetics.* New York: Wiley, 1956.

Barrows, S. Family therapy in Europe: An interview with Maurizio Andolfi. *American Journal of Family Therapy,* 1981, 9, 70–75.

159

160 *Behind the Family Mask*

Bateson, G. *Steps to an ecology of mind.* New York: Ballantine Books, 1972.
Boszormenyi-Nagy, J., & Spark, G. *Invisible loyalties.* New York: Harper & Row, 1973.
Bowen, M. *Family theory in clinical practice.* New York: Aronson, 1978.
Conte, G. *La metafora.* Bari: Laterza, 1981.
Dell, P. The Hopi family and the Aristotelian parents. *Journal of Marital and Family Therapy,* 1980, *6,* 2: 123–130.
Eco, U. *Trattato di semiotica generale.* Milano: Bompiani, 1975.
Farrelly, F., & Brandsma, J. *Provocative therapy.* Fort Collins: Shields Publ., 1974.
Ferreira, A. J. Family myths and homeostasis. *Archives of General Psychiatry,* 1963, *9:* 457–473.
Haley, J. *Strategies of psychotherapy.* New York: Grune & Stratton, 1963.
Haley, J. (Ed.) *Changing families.* New York: Grune & Stratton, 1971.
Haley, J. *Uncommon therapy: The psychiatric techniques of Milton H. Erickson.* New York: W. W. Norton, 1973.
Haley, J. *Problem solving therapy,* San Francisco: Jossey-Bass, 1976.
Hoffman, L. *Foundations of family therapy.* New York: Basic Books, 1981.
Jackson, D. D. The question of family homeostasis. *Psychiat. Quart.,* 1957, *31,* 79–90.
Keith, D., & Whitaker, C. Play therapy: A paradigm for work with families. *Journal of Marital and Family Therapy,* 1981, *7,* 3: 243–254.
Mahler, M. On child psychosis and schizophrenia. *Psychoanalytic Study of the Child,* 1952, *7:* 286–305.
Menghi, P. L'approccio strutturale nella terapia con la famiglia. *Terapia Familiare,* 1977, *1:* 53–76.
Miller, J. C. *Living systems.* New York: McGraw-Hill, 1978.
Minuchin, S. *Families and family therapy.* Cambridge: Harvard Univ. Press, 1974.
Minuchin, S., & Fishman, H. C. *Family therapy techniques.* Cambridge: Harvard Univ. Press, 1981.
Napier, A., & Whitaker, C. *The family crucible.* New York: Harper & Row, 1978.
Nicolò, A. M. L'emploi de la métaphore en thérapie familiale. *Thérapie Familiale,* 1980, *4,* 1.
Nicolò, A., & Saccu, C. L'interaction en situation de crise. Seminario del VI Congresso di Terapia Familiare di Zurigo, 1979.
Piperno, R. La funzione della provocazione nel mantenimento omeostatico dei sistemi rigidi. *Terapia Familiare,* 1979, *5:* 39–50.
Searles, H. Anxiety concerning change as seen in the psychotherapy of schizophrenic patients, with particular reference to the sense of personal identity. *International Journal of Psychoanalysis,* 1961, *42.*
Selvini-Palazzoli, M. Contesto e metacontesto nella psicoterapia della famiglia. *Archivio di Psicologia, Neurologia e Psichiatria,* 1970, *3:* 203–211.
Selvini-Palazzoli, M. Why a long interval between sessions? The therapeutic control of the family-therapist suprasystem. In M. Andolfi and I. Zwerling (Eds.), *Dimensions of family therapy.* New York: Guilford Press, 1980.
Selvini-Palazzoli, M., Boscolo, L., Cecchin, G., & Prata, G. *Paradox and counterparadox.* New York: Aronson, 1978.
Selvini-Palazzoli, M., Boscolo, L., Cecchin, G., & Prata, G. Hypothesizing circular-

ity-neutrality: Three guidelines for the conduction of the session. *Family Process,* 1980, *19,* 1: 3–12.

Stanton, D. Strategic approaches to family therapy. In A. Gurman and D. Kniskern (Eds.), *Handbook of family therapy.* New York: Brunner/Mazel, 1981.

Watzlawick, P., Beavin, J. H., & Jackson, D. D. *Pragmatics of human communication.* New York: W. W. Norton, 1967.

Watzlawick, P., Weakland, L., & Fisch, R. *Change.* New York: Norton, 1974.

Whitaker, C. Psychotherapy of the absurd with a special emphasis on the psychotherapy of aggression. *Family Process,* 1975, *14:* 1–16.

Whitaker, C., & Malone, T. *The roots of psychotherapy.* New York: Brunner/Mazel, 1981.

Index

163